True Stories
New Brunswickers
At War

by Dorothy Dearborn
illustrations by Carol Taylor

Other books by Dorothy Dearborn

Young Adult
The Secret of Pettingill Farms
Avalon Books, New York 1972
The Mystery of Wood Island
Avalon Books 1973

Biographies
Give Me Fifteen Minutes Roy Alward, Havelock
Unipress Limited, Fredericton 1978
Dyslexia Dr. Arthur Chesley, Saint John
Dearborn Group 1992

Anthologies
Willie (A Short Story)
Stubborn Strength by Michael O. Nowlan
Academic Press Canada 1983

Collections
Partners in Progress, New Brunswick
Atlantic Canada-At the Dawn of a New Nation
Windsor Publications Ltd. Burlington, Ontario 1990

Non Fiction
Unsolved New Brunswick Murders 1993
New Brunswick Ghosts, Demons
... and things that go bump in the night 1994
Madness and Murder 1995
Legends, Oddities and Mysteries
including UFO experiences in New Brunswick 1996
New Brunswick's Unsung Heroes 1996
(All above published by Neptune Publishing Company Ltd.)

A paperback original from Neptune Publishing Company Ltd.
First printing September, 1997

The publisher wishes to acknowledge and thank the Department of Municipalities, Culture and Housing for their assistance in this publication.

Canadian Cataloguing in Publication Data

Dearborn, Dorothy 1927–
ISBN 1-896270 - 12 - 3
True Stories New Brunswickers at War
1. World War, 1939-1945 -- Personal narratives, Canadian.
2. Veterans -- New Brunswick -- Biography.
3. New Brunswick -- History, Military. I Title.
D768 .15 . D42 1997   940,54'8171   C97-950154-7

Cover design by Dorothy Dearborn
Illustrations by Carol Taylor

Typesetting by Dearborn Group,
P.O. Box 720.
Hampton, NB

Printed in Canada.

Neptune Publishing Company Ltd.
116 Prince William Street, Box 6941
Saint John, NB E2L 4S4

Acknowledgements

It is virtually impossible to spell out in detail the ways in which so many have helped and encouraged me in the writing of this book.

Much of the research had to be gleaned through reports and chronicles, some of it from one hundred years ago or more. Other material was loaned or verbally presented to me by family members and friends of some of the men whose stories appear in this book, and in some instances from the men themselves. Most are acknowledged within the stories to which they have contributed.

Special thanks must go to Byron O'Leary, 'Mr. Military History of Saint John.' Without his help and kindness this book would lack a great deal of important information ... and I would still be trying to interpret military terminology, I am forever grateful.

Thank you, too, to Rod Logan, Marg Earl and Lou Duffley who guided me in the direction of good stories on a number of occasions.

Teresa MacLean, of Communications Services Veterans Affairs in Charlottetown, was very helpful, as were other VA staff. Photographs of the various medals and ribbons were made available through their kindness.

Bill Scharf assisted me in locating RCAF stories from the Second World War and Louise Turner helped in contacts in the Acadian community. Mrs. C.H. Malchow, Fredericton; Janet Rocher, Petit Rocher and Olive Fournier all played a big role in helping me tell the story of Rocky Fournier and his experience in the Special Operations Executive of the British Secret Service.

Special permission to quote material from the book *Behind Enemy Lines* by Roy MacLaren relevant to Rocky Fournier's story was granted by the University of British Columbia Press.The assistance of Major Harold Skaarup, G2/Intelligence Directing Staff, Tactics School, CTC Gagetown is also gratefully acknowledged.

I am particularly grateful to Mrs. Robert Tooley for her kind permission to quote liberally from her late husband's book *Invicta*, the history of the Carleton and York Regiment in the Second World War. Thanks to Arthur Bishop (son of Canada's famous First World War Flying Ace Billy Bishop) for carte blanche in quoting from his book *Our Bravest and Our Best, The Stories of Canada's Victoria Cross Winners.*

Thanks too, to Jack Veness for permission to quote from the book *The Two Jacks* and to Gordon Fairweather, brother of Jack Fairweather, for his assistance in researching my story, *The Three Jacks.*

While care has been taken to trace the ownership of all copyright material used in the text I, as author, and *Neptune Publishing Company Ltd.*, as publishers welcome any information enabling us to rectify any reference or credit in subsequent editions.

Preface

In the beginning this book was intended to be a small attempt to acknowledge our New Brunswick war heroes: the many men who were recommended to me when I was working on an earlier book, *New Brunswick's Unsung Heroes*. I refrained from using war heroes in that book on the basis that they deserved a book of their own.

This, then, is the book I promised at that time. Obviously it is a book of heroes but the task of selecting representatives of that genre was a daunting one. I can only hope that, in some way, each of the stories offered here will reflect the actions of all those New Brunswickers who have served us so honourably over the years. Each is a hero but no book will ever be big enough to encompass them all.

These are the stories of our parents, our grandparents, our ancestors ... of real people. They are part of our history, our roots. When we read them we don't see in them the same violence that confronts us daily on the television screen.

We believed then, and now, that they were right in their time. We honour those who fought for us.

Today, thanks to that gift of the Twentieth Century called 'Instant Replay' we are treated to a view of the seamier side of life at war on a regular basis. It is not a pretty sight but it, the reality of war, is a reflection of our times and, hopefully, one that eventually will guide us to a world without war.

Even as we, as Canadians, face the reality and the horror of war, a part of us continues to look back to a time when fighting for one's country was perceived as an honourable cause, carried out with dignity and pride. Perhaps it was no less bloody and possibly no more honourable than it is today but we saw it differently.

It was the stuff heroes are made of.

Dorothy Dearborn
Hampton, NB.
July 22, 1997

Contents

Medals and Ribbons

Some Acadians Were Busy Behind Enemy Lines

SOE, the Special Operations Executive, was a small, tough British secret service; a dirty tricks department set up in July of 1940. Its job was to support and stimulate resistance in occupied countries. It exercised vast influence on the war, not just on every front but throughout the world.

SOE secret agents operated both in the war sector and within the halls of power ... whether those halls belonged to friends and allies or to the enemy and their friends and allies.

"Like any other body of warriors, they made some fearful mistakes. They also displayed, to a most unusual degree, the highest qualities of character, courage, and devotion to freedom." (From the cover of *SOE The Special Operations Executive* 1940 to 1946 by M.R.D. Foot)

While we may know a considerable amount about New Brunswick men and women in the regular forces during the two world wars and the war in Korea, we know precious little about those New Brunswickers who served the cause of freedom in a different way. Those who volunteered to be secret agents.

As far as I can determine two Acadians from New Brunswick were among the 28 Canadians who were dropped into France during 1944. Some of them worked behind enemy lines both in German-occupied Europe and later in Japa- nese-occupied Asia. Their roles were to support the efforts of the under- ground and resist- ance movements, made up of local peo- ple fighting against Fascist powers who were trying to take over their countries. Of these 28, eight were killed and several became prisoners of war.

Canadian secret agents came from three groups: French Canadians/ Acadians, im- migrants from Italy and Eastern Europe and Chinese Ca- nadians. They served in France, Yugoslavia, Hungary, Italy, Burma, Malaya and Sarwak between 1939 and 1945.

Unlike their counterparts in the regular military forces, they received no public recognition for their ex- tremely dangerous work. They had no rousing send- offs before going into battle, the name of their game was secrecy. The outcome of their battles depended on total secrecy and individual acts of courage.

William Stevenson, master spy and hero of the book and later the movie *A Man Called Intrepid* was a Canadian. He headed up the SOE (better known as the British Secret Service).

Of the 14,000 heroes who worked within this far-reaching organization I have so far identified two New Brunswickers. An Acadian miner and truck driver from Petit Rocher, Joseph Ernest Fournier; and a Carleton and York Regiment infantryman, Ferdinand Joseph LaPointe.   Detailed information on LaPointe's work in France is sparse but, reading from the chronicles of his compatriots it appears he was parachuted into southern France Aug. 16, 1944 carrying the rank of Lieutenant. He, like Fournier, was a radio operator on an inter-Allied mission, the seventh and final Canadian from SOE's training camp in Algeria, to be parachuted into occupied France. He was there for six weeks, until Sept. 28.

Outside of this bare bones information all that is known of LaPointe is that he died in California in 1965.

Rocky Fournier wasn't a big man but he was tough, resilient, smart and fluently bilingual

Olive Fournier knew little, if anything, of her husband's role during the Second World War. But London native Olive Wallington was a WAAF (Women's Auxiliary Air Force) serving with the RAF Signals and accepted that whatever her husband was doing had to be done, for the good of the free world.

Now, over 80 years of age, she still admits to knowing very little of his military career, save what has been written over the years and is retained in the archives of his regiment, Régiment de Trois-Riviéres (12 AR) in Trois Riviéres, Québec.

Petit-Rocher-born Joseph Ernest "Rocky" Fournier enlisted in the Royal Canadian Corps of Signals in Toronto in April of 1942. Prior to that time he had worked at the Pickle Crow gold mine north of Lake Superior.

The enlisting officer had been impressed with him. "It was an initial impression which proved valid throughout Fournier's varied and taxing military career in both Europe and Asia," wrote Roy MacLaren, one time Ontario Member of Parliament and author of the book *Canadians Behind Enemy Lines.*[1]

Early in 1944, while attached to New Brunswick's North Shore Regiment in Italy, Fournier was recruited for SOE training in Algeria.

On Aug. 12 in the same year he was dropped by

parachute into southern France, one of a nine-member team of Canadians, sent to link the resistance with the Allied forces which were to land in southern France three days later.

Pauline Vanier and her husband George, who was in Algiers as Canadian minister to de Gaulle's Free French government operating from there, visited the Canadians during their training. On Aug. 19, 1944 Mme. Vanier wrote the following letter to Fournier's mother:

Office of the Representative of Canada
to the
French Committee of National Liberation

Algiers, 19th. August 1944

Dear Mrs. Fournier,
I hope that you received my letter sent to you about four weeks ago in which I told you about meeting your son? He has seen (sic) left Algiers to follow the course that I told you about. He has arrived safely and is very well indeed. But as you know he will not be allowed to write to you for a bit, so you must'nt (sic) worry about him. It wont (sic) be long now though I am sure before he will be able to write; just have a little more patientce (sic) .....
The news is everywhere so good now that we can really hope that this horrible war will soon be over ....
With my best regards
Yours sincerely,
(signed Pauline Vanier)
(Mrs. George Vanier)

MacLaren[1] describes Fournier as a man who had, from the age of seventeen, lived a hard life in New Brunswick and in northern Ontario and who, "despite his short, slight stature, was a tough, resilient man, accustomed to improvising and living in the rough – good qualifications for a guerrilla."

He and team-mate Ben Hunter were parachuted into France together and, MacLaren said, "the contrast between the two could hardly have been greater."

Hunter, tall and dark, was an urbane McGill graduate from Montreal who had been commissioned in the Royal Artillery (British Army) following a prewar career as a surveyor.

Their leader, D.E.F. Green, had served a prewar prison sentence and went on to teach lock-forcing and safe-cracking to SOE trainees in southern England. He was so eager to see action before the fighting ended that he finally persuaded headquarters to let him go on a mission. He was not disappointed.

"In Hunter he had an able deputy and in Fournier a radio operator who was as adaptable and skilful as was the leader himself," MacLaren said.

Their ultimate destination was the Haute-Savoie, a wooded mountainous area south of Geneva bordering on Switzerland and Italy. There the resistance, operating from the mountains, had long been involved in continuing skirmishes with the enemy.

The Haute-Savoie offered little hope of a secure reception for the allies because of the active and mobile German garrison located there. The mission was dropped close to the village of Seyne, nearer the Mediterranean in the Basses Alpes. Their orders were to make their way somehow through the French Alps and to then spread out through the Haute-Savoie area to act as a link between the local, very active underground and the Allied headquarters in Algiers.

There was concern in the mission over the quality of the parachutes from Algiers.The problem with the parachutes lay in the shortage of silk, or the more recent nylon, used for the parachutes. They had resorted to the use of heavy cotton parachutes made in Egypt, which frequently tangled, did not open, or otherwise failed to deliver the precious loads of supplies and ammunition intact.

The cannisters containing the radio equipment were frequently damaged on landing. As a result, initial contact with Algiers was sometimes delayed because of damage to the wireless batteries. Fournier's and Hunter's team was faced with this problem as well as with the difficulty of transmitting from mountain valleys far from receiving stations, which doubled their problems.

Somewhere and somehow Fournier succeeded in finding new acid for his set of batteries, recharged them and, within four days of landing, began transmission, enabling the mission to receive air drops and coordinate attacks on retreating German columns.

On Sept 4 Hunter hastened the German garrison at St. Miche-en-Maurienne on its way by leading an attack on the telegraph fort covering the approaches to the town. It only took seven rounds of mortar fire for the team to silence the German's guns. In all, of the 60 Germans in strong positions, 22 were killed and the Germans were forced to withdraw.

Of the 25 Canadians who volunteered to go behind enemy lines in France, seven were captured and executed.

The team successfully struck at German troops throughout their trek through the Alps and eventually met up with Montgomery's 21st Army.

Ironically, at this point, Olive Fournier says her husband told her the Canadians were ordered, by de Gaulle, to be out of France in 24 hours or risk capture and punishment. Years later, when de Gaulle made his famous *Vive le Quebec libre!* speech in Montreal his driver arrived at the Fournier home and delivered the Croix de Guerre and - Palm, of the French Resistance. There was no ceremony, just a package delivered to the door. Fournier had earlier been advised that he had been mentioned in dispatches from the British War office.

"Canadians," MacLaren[1] said, "coming from remarkably varied backgrounds, risked their lives in the land of their ancestors or in a land which they regarded as sharing the same transcendental values of their own homeland–the antithesis of Nazi ideology. To defeat Hitler's brutish regime and to help restore Europe to the mainstream of its traditions was to them worth all the many risks of clandestine warfare."

Next: Burma
and the jungle

Rocky Fournier was one of 10 Canadians, of the 17 who survived their hazardous service in occupied France, to volunteer once again for SOE operations. This time in southeast Asia.

The SOE was known as Force 136 in Asia. Life for the secret agent there was quite different from what he had experienced in France. There was no solid, well-

When Burma beckoned Rocky Fournier dropped behind the Japanese lines to train jungle troops and, eventually, to rescue 250 allied troops lost in the jungle during the battle for Burma.

• • • • • • • • • • • • • • • • • • • •

organized group of local people, such as the French Resistance movement, with whom SOE agents could align themselves. Most of the native peoples in the Japanese-occupied countries were either indifferent or antagonistic towards the Europeans and the SOE had to enlist the support of local communist guerrillas in the fight against the Japanese.

In February of 1945 SOE learned that arrangements had been negotiated whereby the Communist Party placed its Malayan People's Anti-Japanese Army under the general operational orders of Lord Mountbatten's Southeast Asia Command, in return for British instructors with arms, explosives, money, medicine and other supplies. For this reason SOE decided to support local communists against the Japanese invaders. In August that year they sent an all Chinese-Canadian force of agents into Malaya to fight side-by-side with communist guerillas.

In the meantime the French Canadians, among them Joseph Fournier, took several months of training at SOE's Eastern Warfare School where they learned about jungle survival and local languages and customs. In April of 1945 eight of them, including Fournier, were parachuted into Burma as part of Operation Character in the Karenni Highlands.

The focus of the war in Burma at this time was a final assault on Rangoon by seaborne and parachute attack, scheduled for May 2 before the Monsoons, and a drive for a land attack by the 14th Army at the same time. The 14th Army had less than six weeks to get there and Lord Mountbatten ordered the general to "take all risks" to ensure their objectives.

As the 14th Army moved southward the Japanese were pushed back into the hills flanking the Sittang valley and there the Karens, people originally from eastern Tibet and loyal to the British, awaited them.

Because of their skin colour and their inability to speak the local languages, F136 could not move about the country disguised as locals, as they had in France. They had to operate away from the main population centres, usually in the jungle where they faced new dangers, among them a variety of tropical diseases. Their "cover" was a green jungle uniform worn with high canvas boots and an Australian type bush hat.

They proceeded to link up with the Karens and began ambushing Japanese troops, who were attempting to escape across the mountains into Thailand.

Fournier lived with the tribesmen and took part in the ambushes and provided the essential radio link with SOE's Burma section headquarters in Calcutta.

McLaren[1] quotes one of the students, who passed through the jungle training, describing in detail how they learned to live in the jungle by moving and living in it.

"We learned how to carve out paths where no paths were, to fashion our own snug habitations, to extract drinking water from what looked like black slimy ooze, to eat strange fruits and stranger flesh, to conceal ourselves so effectively that a man might approach to within a yard of our hiding-place without suspecting we were there.

"In time we could read the jungle like a book ... we could identify jungle smells and developed the quivering awareness of the beasts and reptiles ... but we were still afraid in the jungle ... the man without fear there is the man without caution."

They had learned to make their fear to work for them.

Rocky Fournier and Paul-Emile Thibeault (from Montreal) dropped in to reinforce teams in the Hyena area of Burma. Fortunately, the village head man where they served spoke a little English and the Karens were willing students of clandestine warfare. The men shared the same diet of wild rice, wild pork and chicken and the endless rain as the Monsoons hit.

Thibeault continued to instruct the Karens in the use of explosives while Fournier provided the essential wireless link with SOE's Burma section headquarters in Calcutta. The incessant dampness caused endless problems for him in maintaining his radio and its generator but his success was duly noted by British Lt. Col. H.W.

Howell who wrote:

"I should like to call attention to the good services rendered by Lt. Fournier. He is a first-class operator and technician; he is capable of keeping any equipment in order. I consider him one of the best and most useful officers under my command.

Howell generally took Fournier with him as he visited as many of the Force 136 teams as the terrain would allow. Using an aerial on a long bamboo pole, Fournier kept both the Hyena headquarters and Calcutta informed of what Howell and he had found.

But Fournier was not content to be only a radio operator. He went into action from one of the outstations commanded by a young British prewar commercial artist named Wilson. Their part of Hyena was particularly dangerous.

"Wilson had started off with a few spectacular ambushes along the main track, and then his entire area had been overrun and for a while he and Fournier had to go into hiding in the jungle and exist the best they could on bamboo shoots and roots."

Once the 14th army succeeded in capturing Rangoon and the Japanese were either dead or struggling across the Karenni hills into Thailand, Fournier, fighting off recurring dysentery and malaria, proceeded to walk out of the jungle. Under his command a unit of more than two hundred men, most of them British and Americans who had been cut off from their fighting units and were hiding in the jungle, walked to join the 14th Army at Toungoo, a major town on the Sittang. From there Fournier was flown to hospital in Calcutta and, when well enough to travel, was sent home to Canada.

For the rest of his life Fournier would suffer the results of the illnesses that plagued him as a result of his involvement in Force 136 in Burma, his final assignment.

On returning to Canada he and Olive lived for a short time in Bathurst where he worked for the federal Employment Office before settling in Trois Riviéres, Que. where he was in the insurance business until his death in 1967, at the age of 50.

Historians describe people like Fournier as "rugged individualists, idealistic and willing to put their lives on the line to defend their ideals."

To Olive and his two sons he was simply "a wonderful man."

[1] This excerpt is reprinted with permission of the Publisher from *Canadians Behind Enemy Lines*, 1939-1945 by Roy MacLaren Vancouver: The University of British Columbia, 1981. All rights reserved by the Publisher.

Permission is also extended to non-profit organizations who may, in future, wish to transcribe the text in Braille/large-type/audio editions, without charge, solely for use by those who are physically and mentally challenged.

True Stories New Brunswickers at War

This four-legged heroine became a 'Freewoman of Hampton'

Alas, there is but one story in this book that relates the story of a female and the important wartime role she played in battle. Not because there weren't brave New Brunswick women in wartime ... it's just that to date I have had little luck in finding their specific stories. The one exception, while female, is not a woman ... she is a pony named Princess Louise.

Hers is one of my all-time favourite war stories, one Hampton friends and neighbours, proud members of the 8th Canadian Hussars (Princess Louise's) delighted in telling.

Princess Louise was born during the Second World War in the hills of Italy, in the midst of battle. The 8th (N.B.) Hussars were fighting their way north with the 5th Armoured Regiment when they found her, still wobbling on newborn legs, trying to nurse from her mortally wounded mother.

The men of the regiment were no strangers to livestock, many of them were from the farming area of Hampton and Sussex in the Kennebecasis Valley of New Brunswick. They were determined that the brave little foal should live. With loving hands and arms they tended to the cuts she suffered, tied off her umbilical cord then virtually carried her to their surgery where they nursed her like a child.

It is no mean feat to care for a newborn in war time but care for her they did as they fought their way across Europe to the successful end of Nazi tyranny there. She rewarded their love with a spirit of her own, often giving them cause for laughter when tears would have prevailed and, in many ways, doing her share as a bona fide member of the regiment.

A fitting mascot for a cavalry regiment, Princess Louise went into battle with the troops. As a member of the 8th Hussars regiment she earned her campaign ribbons in Italy, France and Germany as well as the CVSM (Canadian Voluntary Service Medal). She wore these, along with three wound stripes, on her saddle pads below her regimental shoulder patch, all of which was subsequently duly approved during inspection by no less a personage than Field Marshall Montgomery himself.

For three years the game little pony had marched or ridden (in her own private truck) across Europe to Holland and thence to England where she was left in the care of the Royal Army Veterinary Corps. She was considered to be "absent with leave" until her regiment could make arrangement for her to join them in Canada.

This proved to be more difficult than anticipated. Red tape abounded. The active service part of the regiment was disbanded on Feb. 15 and regrouped to peacetime status, to all intents and purposes "the family was together again" … with one exception. Princess Louise was cooling her hoofs overseas and her regiment missed her and wanted her "home" with them.

Everyone who owned a pullable string pulled it, in high place and low until finally the little mare set sail … and Saint John, Rothesay and Hampton set out a welcome mat worthy of royalty.

Her first civic reception was on King Street East in Saint John where she was greeted by Brigadier D.R. Agnew, officer commanding of Military District No.7, and Mayor James D. McKenna who introduced the "Princess" to the citizens over a loud speaker system, supplied by military headquarters.

A parade, headed by No. 4 Army Band, under Bandmaster Percy Belyea, playing *Road to the Isles* and followed by Princess Louise, escorted by a guard of honor composed of veterans of the unit and armoured vehicles, marched from King Street East down Sydney Street, along Union and Charotte, around King's Square and back to King Street East where a number of small children had the supreme honour of riding the famous pony.

The Princess then began her journey to what was to become her new home in Hampton, site of the unit headquarters. John Allison, who owned the Gilbert's Lane Riding School supplied transportation for her. On the way she stopped at Rothesay where a throng of school children, given leave from their studies for the occasion, welcomed her to Kings County. She arrived in Hampton at 4:30 p.m.

It was in Hampton that the climax to her 16,000 mile ship and rail journey took place. She was introduced to the villagers by Lt.-Col. G.H.R. Ross, former commanding officer of the unit. This was followed immediately by the reading of her biography from the balcony of the county court house by R. Fred Pickett, the county secretary.

She was then presented with a bale of hay, a bag of oats and a shovel and fork by Dr.V.A. Snow following which the reception concluded with a dramatic presentation: A "Certificate of Naturalization" by Magistrate Arthur J. Kelly.

This certificate was of far reaching influence:

Know all men by these here present (viz. one bale of hay and one bag of oats) that the Royal Lady, hereinafter known as Princess Louise, is hereby made and proclaimed a citizen of the great Dominion of Canada and a freewoman of the Village of Hampton (including Hampton Station) and as such is entitled to roam at will over hill and vale in that community and to devour and partake of that which she pleaseth, whether it be from carefully tended garden or from the bursting warehouse of Henry Sharp and in addition may at her discretion find and take lodging wheresoever she desireth, whether it be in private home, public building of Nos. 1 & 2 firesheds.

"And furthermore let it be known to all and sundry that should the said princess require at any time succour, aid, help or any other form of assistance, it shall be the bounden duty of any and all citizens of the aforementioned community to afford such assistance within a reasonable time or ear the full penalty of the law ..."

Princess Louise now lies at rest in Hampton. Her memorial, erected by the Hampton Branch of the Royal Canadian Legion notes her birth date, 1944 and the year of her death, 1973. It also commemorates her daughter, Princess Louise II, 1954-1981, who took over mascot duties in the regiment from her mother.

The monument shares space with Hampton's War Memorial in the small Memorial Park at entrance to the Hampton Community Club. On Remembrance Day, Princess Louise, like her fellows of the regiment, is also remembered with a wreath of poppies.

Distinguished Service Cross

Originally designated the Conspicuous Service Cross (1901-1914), the Distinguished Service Cross was awarded to naval personnel, from Warrant Officer to Lieutenant, for the performance of meritorious or distinguished services before the enemy.

In 1939, Commanders and Lieutenant-Commanders were also made eligible for the DSC. Members of the air force or army serving with the fleet were also eligible.

'Bars' were awarded for the performance of subsequent acts of service before the enemy. The slip-on bar is silver, with a crown in the centre, and is convex at the ends of the arms. At the time of the Second World War, the year the bar was awarded was engraved on the back.

Description: A plain silver cross pattée[1], convex and 1.5625 inches across.

Obverse: The obverse shows the Royal Cypher on the circular central medallion surmounted by a crown. The cyphers GV, GVI and EIIR have been used for Canadian awards.

Reverse: The reverse is plain, with the year of the award engraved on the lower arm.

Mounting : A large ring (0.75 inches in diameter)

is linked to a small ring welded to the top arm.

Ribbon: The ribbon is 1.375 inches wide and consists of three equal stripes: navy blue, white, and navy blue. A rosette is worn in undress to signify a bar.

Dates: The award was originally established in June 1901 as the Conspicuous Service Cross and changed to the Distinguished Service Cross in October, 1914.

[1] *pattée means widening of the cross arms toward the ends.*

The Brock Family ...
among the Navy's finest

Citations leave much to be desired in terms of portraying the actual story behind honours awarded and the persons who earned them. Such was the case when I came across the name "Brock" while perusing one of Byron O'Leary's many books on militaria of all persuasions.

The citation was for John Brock, Lieut. Commander and simply said he had been awarded the *Distinguished Service Cross* as of Aug. 14, 1945: For service in action against enemy submarines.

Since the home of the said John Brock was in nearby Rothesay my curiosity was piqued. I took to the telephone book. My reward came swiftly in stories of not one but two men.

John and Fred Brock, were both Lieutenant-Commanders, one with the Canadian Navy the other with the British navy. Both were "Skippers" of those mighty little floating tigers ... the corvettes that fought off everything from submarines, E-boats and dive bombers to human torpedoes in the Second World War.

Their job was the far ranging defence of the convoys crossing the Atlantic; the defence of Great Britain from German U-Boats; the protection of the Allied fleet during the raid on Dieppe; and the subsequent invasion of Europe leading to the final defeat of Hitler and all he stood for.

Their exploits offer the makings of a television series that could rival any American offering when it comes to riveting excitement, heroism and leadership.

According to Evelyn Brock, Fred Brock's widow, the two brothers were very close and great friends all their lives.

Fred started "fooling around with sail boats" as a child and had been in the RCNVR (the navy's volunteer reserve) for five years when war broke out in 1939. At that time he took command of *HMCS Saint John* (now *Brunswicker*).

When the Royal Navy asked for volunteers from Canada in 1940, following the disaster at Dunquerque, Fred heard the call and spent the rest of the war on loan to the Royal Navy. He served on five warships in all and on two occasions got vessels and their crews back to port after they struck mines.

When he returned to New Brunswick in 1945, for the first time in five years, a Royal Canadian Navy press release pointed out that he "has more action behind him than most seagoing men would meet in a lifetime.

The *Distinguished Service Cross*, presented to him by King George VI at Buckingham Palace was awarded for "Outstanding initiative in the defence of the British assault area and offensive and defensive patrols off the enemy-held coast of France."

The news release went on to say that the citation barely touched on Brocks career. He was mentioned in dispatches for his part in sinking a German U-boat in the Bay of Biscay in the summer of 1943. The same day his boat assisted in sinking a second U-boat. Wreckage of the first came to the surface after being heavily depth-charged. The second one was blown to the top and rammed by another sloop and then disappeared.

"But we hit the jackpot another day when the group got two U-boats, and some aircraft we were working with got another one, all in the same day. They were all sunk by depth charges."

He was recommended for command after serving in the famous RN support group under Capt. F.J. Walker who, it was said, "did more to end the U-boat menace in the North Atlantic than any other officer."

It was when he took over command of the Captain class U.S. Frigate *HMS Duff* and entered into the thick of night patrols off the British sector of the Normandy beaches that his reputation as a fighting skipper grew by leaps and bounds.

The frontispiece to the book *MacNamara's Band*, by the *Duff*'s radio officer, Bernard Griffiths, reads:

"She was not a ship that hit the headlines, but to her crew she was a happy ship and they wanted no other. She certainly gave a good account of herself. She fought mainly in the crowded home waters; her enemies were the Luftwaffe, the lurking U-boats, the high speed, quick firing E-boats and lastly, the deadly mines. Her life was not a long one, but she managed to take a heavy toll of the enemy, and when at last her end came, she managed to land her crew safely ashore."

In one 24 hour period the *Duff* took on no fewer than 15 motor torpedo boats (E-boats), submarines, aircraft and the manned (human) torpedoes that hid among the waves beneath the radar, biding their time until ready to attack at close range.

"We operated off LeHarve and Cherbourg, cooperating with coastal forces," Brock said later, "and ran into at least 15 hot engagements with E-boats, one of which the frigate shot up."

Brock and his crew also captured three of the

human torpedos.

In *MacNamara's Band*, Bernard Griffiths simply notes that his commanding officer, Fred Brock, was a young Canadian Lieutenant when he first met him. In the autographed copy of the book, given to Brock, he says:

"To the Skipper, With deep respect and best wishes from one of the ship's company."

Griffiths describes *H.M.S. Duff*, as "a steam-turbine-driven ship, of all welded fabrication, displacing about fifteen hundred tons. Her armament consisted of three, three-inch guns and twin "Bofors," the latter being in the position usually described as "X" gun. Her secondary armament consisted of six Oerlikon guns. She also carried depth charges and a new anti-submarine weapon known as a Hedgehog. This was situated aft of "A" gun and consisted of twenty four metal tubes, inclined towards the bows, arranged in four rows of six. Each tube contained an electrical circuit which fired a bomb-shaped missile that fitted over it. The whole arrangement could be trained by tilting the tubes to port or starboard, so that the missiles were fired to either side of the bows and exploded under water when in contact with a U-boat."

It was around June 3, 1944, Griffiths says, "when the Skipper got his half-stripe and the ship's record, *MacNamara's Band* arrived on board ...

"... At the end of her commission the *Duff* had proved to be a happy and efficient ship. By this time the ship's company had been welded into a family. Cliche thought that is, it is the only word that I can think of to describe us–and this was entirely due to Lieutenant-Commander Brock. He had a good understanding of the lower deck and regarded each of us as

It was around June 3, 1944, when the Skipper got his half-stripe and the ship's record, MacNamara's Band arrived on board ...at the end of her commission the Duff had proved to be a happy and efficient ship. By this time the ship's company had been welded into a family. Cliche though that is, it is the only word that I can think of to describe us–and this was entirely due to Lieutenant-Commander Brock.

• •

an individual. He was the only Commanding Officer, to my knowledge, who, when ordering a rating to do something apart from the efficient running of the ship, would say 'Please' and would thank him when it was accomplished. He knew every one of the ship's company by name.

"The ship's record was his idea. He wanted a record that could be played over the loud hailer on entering or leaving harbour. His choice was the Mills Brothers' recording of *MacNamara's Band*. Records at that time were difficult to obtain, so we were playing the Andrews Sisters' version of *In the Navy* until it arrived just before D-Day.

"Many ships played records, of course. They were good for morale. It set the ship apart from any other and drew attention to it. But I believe MacNamara's Band was the best one of all. The words, 'Although we're small in numbers we're the finest in the land' appealed to us. We *were* small in numbers and, after D-Day, on entering harbour after a night's patrol we felt we were 'the finest in the land.'."

I doubt that Griffiths book is still in print, the one lent to me by Evelyn Brock was published in England in 1960. It's a good read and I have taken the liberty of quoting a few passages here. I believe they faithfully portray "the way it was" in the war-torn days of 1944 when the battle raged over the land, sea and air of western Europe and Great Britain.

A wonderfully descriptive passage describes how the vessels on patrol worked as a team to both defeat the enemy and support each other throughout the long nights.

"Fox Love Two, this is Fox Love One. There are five echoes at about 040, 11,000 yards from you, on a course of 360. Probably E-boats. Vector Vector 010, George George 28. Over."

"Fox Love Two One. Roger."

"Two Two. Roger."

"Two Three. Roger."

On the bridge, the Skipper watched three dark shadows detach themselves from the blackness astern and vanish to starboard, the rumble of their accelerating engines dwarfing the noises of our own ship.

"Right," said Lieutenant Harry. "Now for Fox Love

Three. Tell them to steer 310–what speed?"–he turned to the Control Officer–"25?"

"Yes that'll bring them ahead of us and ahead of the E-boats on the course we hope they'll steer."

"Right, Sparks. Twenty-five knots."

"Fox Love Three, This is Fox Love One. Vector Vector 310, George George 25. Over."

So our second group of boats left us to take up their position ...

... ... The control officer looked across at Lieutenant Harry. "If all goes well, Fox Love Two should make contact in about eight minutes."

"Lieutenant Harry nodded. "I'll tell the bridge."

"How far will they be from us when they do engage?" the Skipper enquired.

"About 12,000 yards."

"And if they turn as you expect, how long will it be before they're within 3,000 yards of us?

"Twelve minutes, sir."

And so the pattern was set. The enemy, steering north towards the convoy routes, was rapidly being overhauled by Fox Love Two, who hoped to turn them to the west, so that the Duff, steering a parallel course to the E-Boats, but at a distance of five miles, would intercept them on the new course, while Fox Love Three was approaching the course more from the westward.

It was quiet on the bridge, save for the ship's noises, the sea, the wind in the halyards and aerials, and the noise and vibration of the engines. Although it was expected, it was a shock when tracks of a tracer arched through the darkness towards the horizon. The Skipper spoke down the Plot Room voice pipe.

"They're engaging now. Send a signal to C-inC: 'Am engaging enemy in position ——' you've got that down there."

"Yes sir."

"But we already knew that the boats had joined issue. They were talking to each other over the R/T and the stammer of their armament was drowning their voices at times.

"Tony, Bob, this is Chief. Can you see them?"

Tony here. Yes, can see them in your tracer. Going through now."

"Chief, watch out! There's one behind you."

"Chief. Roger." And through his microphone came the chatter of Lewis guns.

The boats, going like steam engines, roared through the enemy line, their guns firing at a range of thirty yards. The flat trajectory of the E-boats' tracer was like thin, vicious wires through which the boats would have to crash their way. The third boat, Bob, crossed the wake of the last E-boat as it dropped a depth charge. It came through the fountain of water apparently unscathed.

The boats, once through the line, turned on a parallel course and engaged again until the enemy did what we wanted them to do and broke off the engagement by turning to the west..........

.... But they didn't remain engaged for long: the E-boats accelerated violently and the boats lost them.

But that was not the end of the night's actions. Fox Love Two had suffered hits on the hull and all the ships worked together to get him within the protection of Duff's guns. While they worked at this sharp eyes were still focused on the radar and an echo was located 500 hundred yards from the ship.

Below the bridge, "B" gun swung easily on the electric pumps.

The phone number at the gun spoke: " 'B' gun, with star shell, load, load, load."

The loading numbers heaved the loading tray to the open breech. The tray worker pulled the lever as the rammer pushed the shell into the breech.

Phone number "B" gun: "Shoot! Shoot! Shoot!"

Crash!

And again.

And again.

In the Plot Room the stench of cordite drifted in.

Ahead, three balls of light drifted down, illuminating the black shapes moving across our bows.

"A" gun phone number spoke: "'A' gun, with Direct Action shell, load, load, load."

The loading numbers sprang into action..................

.... Round after round crashed out. Another three rounds from "B" gun augmented the waning illumination. White fountains rose around the black shapes. They maintained their course for a while but the accuracy of the fire was too great. Just as they turned, a shell burst alongside one E-boat and seemed to knock it sideways. It stopped and turned broadside on, but then recovered its course and followed its colleagues, drawing gradually out of range.

The Skipper spoke gloomily down the voice pipe.

"Lost them. Any chance of the other boats making contact?"

"No, sir. They're away out of range. Still, we did damage one."

"Yes." The Skipper brightened. "That's so. You'd better give me a course to regain our patrol position. ....

.... And so, eventually we picked up Fox Love Two and resumed our patrol. It was quiet in the Plot Room but we still felt the elation that pervaded the *ship.*

Shortly afterwards we learned via the Wireless Office that the E-boats had been engaged again by the destroyers Sioux and Athabaskan on a patrol nearer the beachhead and had suffered further damage.

That same night four echoes on the Radar alerted the Duff once more.

"Give me a course and speed." said the Skipper. "And send a first sighting report to Portsmouth."

Soon it was realized that there were no fewer than seven echoes within a range of 11,500 yards.

"Sparks, tell the office to send: 'Seven E-boats sighted 239 degrees Poite de Barfleur 16 miles. Course 010, speed 22 knots."

Keeping *Fox Love Two*, with its lame duck from the earlier encounter, tucked into relative safety behind them the *Duff* and its escort MTRs (Motor Torpedo Boats) set off at full speed to once more engage the enemy.

The enemy is not far off and we are racing to intercept again. Each mind is occupied with its private thoughts. Who can tell what our luck will be this time? Steam scalds, the tortured metal mutilates, and men are like rats in a trap when the sea crashed through a broken ship. An engine room is no place to be when a torpedo strikes. But no one moves and no one thinks of moving.

From Georgie Lowe: "There are now eight echoes bearing 140, range 9,000 yards."

Eight E-boats patrolling. Looking for trouble.

Once again the guns are ready, the muzzles tracking, following Gunnery Control.

Echoes bearing 135, range 8,000 yards."

Echoes bearing 130, range 7,000 yards."

Still waiting, still tense.
"Echoes bearing 125, range 6,000 yards"
Then suddenly ————
Echoes bearing 122, range 5,500 yards."
The E-boats are turning towards us!" ....
The Skipper speaks. "What speed are they doing?"
"About 30 knots, sir."

The guns are blaring as the Duff churns on full speed ahead when suddenly from the port lookout:

"Torpedo track! Red Fifty , sir"
The Skipper spoke down the wheelhouse voice pipe.
"Hard a-port."
"Hard a-port, sir," came the Cox'n's unruffled voice.
"Wheels hard a-port, sir."

The deck canted violently and on the empty mess decks unsecured articles clattered to the deck and rolled to the port side. The ship came round as the torpedo bubbled viciously past the bows.

"Midships."
"Midships, sir. Wheel amidships, sir."
"Starboard 30."
"Starboard 30, sir. 30 of starboard wheel on, sir.
"Steady."
"Steady on 010, sir."

.... *The Skipper disregarded the vanishing torpedo track. The after guns were able to ear on the E-boats again. The range was closing and now the bow-chaser and the Bofors and even the port Oerlikons were firing.*

With all the armament firing, one discovers an orchestra of sound. The hysterical, the urgently hysterical chatter of the Oerlikons, the ear-splittingly sharp crash of the 3-inch supported in the background by the monotonous, almost unhurried Bofors and the clockwork-

like fire of the pom-pom blend in a symphony of defiance.

Then, amid those phosphorescent splashes, one of the low shapes swung out of line and blossomed flame as it listed over. The remainder turned away to escape the terrible fire-power bent upon them.

The Duff altered course and surged after them, still firing. But the angle soon prevented the bofors and Y gun firing and the three forward guns only were trained on the E-boats. As we passed the wreck of the E-boat, faint voices were heard in the water and a few bobbing heads and waving arms swept by us.

The Skipper glanced at them. " Slip them a Carley float," he ordered, and then: "Plot, get one of the MTBs to search for survivors.

Slowly the E-boats crept out of range and the pom-pom ceased firing.

The *Duff* ceased firing to allow the MTBs to move in and they managed to damage two more E-boats before the enemy disengaged and the *Duff* returned to its patrol duties.

The tension eased and the rest of the night was one of steady plodding up and down the patrol lines.

.... *Dawn came creeping over the empty sea. No ships were visible except ourselves and the MTBs tumbling along in our wake. We stopped and took off seven German survivors from the MTB and bundled them quickly below to the tiller flat under guard............*

............*"Bridge, plot," from the voice pipe.*
"Plot," I answered.
"Close down Radar and R/T."

....

............*On the mess deck everything was quiet and I crawled into my bunk and slept till breakfast time. Al-*

though I could have slept again, I stayed up until we sailed into the Solent, our pennant numbers standing at the yardarm, MacNamara's Band blaring from the loud hailer as usual. ....

.... The Skipper went ashore to make his report and we settled down to harbour routine again.

A close call ...
followed by a fond farewell

After some very heavy battles the Duff limped into port and was ordered into the dockyard for minor repairs. Paul Breakhall, an RN officer who served with Brock told Mrs. Brock that everyone was exhausted and quite shaken. Her husband, however, ordered a lifeboat to be fitted with sails and proceeded to sail around the area for an hour or two. The entire crew stood on deck and watched him with astonishment.

Breakhall said it did wonders for the crew's morale. Later, Mrs. Brock questioned her husband about the incident. He laughed and confessed, "I really did it for myself. I just needed to be alone for awhile!"

There were those among the crew at this time who thought the refit might mean the end of their harrowing nightly vigils.

"The obstacle to any likelihood of this 'buzz' becoming fact was the Skipper," Griffiths said in his book. "Knowing him as we now did, it seemed very unlikely that we would return there (to patrol off Ireland) if he had his way, while any chance of fighting remained."

Back on patrol again the *Duff* and the other vessels were subject to more than the vagaries of the E-boats. The frequently sewn enemy mines were taking their toll as were the hitherto unknown human torpedoes.

One night, just as the *Duff* made its way out to

sea the frigate *Trollope* was torpedoed within sight of the crew. As the *Duff* helped with the rescue of survivors a lookout on the bridge spotted an object some distance away.

The Skipper looked, immediately ordered full speed ahead and alerted the quarterdeck to stand by for a depth charge attack.

Leading Stoker Brown, who had just come up from the engine room, saw the object from the waist. A Perspex, semicircular dome was visible, just awash in the choppy sea. He, and everyone, watched fascinated as we raced towards it. It was a human torpedo, the pilot clearly visible as we got nearer. Here was one of those deadly craft of which we had heard rumours but which we had never seen yet. It was probably one of the craft that had launched their torpedoes at the two minesweepers.

The Duff, still increasing speed, swept past it and, with a puff of smoke, a wobbling cylindrical object rose from the quarterdeck in parabolic flight, plunged into the sea and exploded just below the surface with a jarring crash. The surface shuddered and then boiled up in a huge white tower of foam, hiding the human torpedo. When the water had subsided, the torpedo had gone. Almost certainly it had been destroyed, but as no one had actually seen its end, we were credited with a 'probable.'

This was, I believe, the first really successful sortie that the torpedoes had carried out, but from then on they were to become a very real danger to the beachhead.

The human torpedos consisted of nothing more than a torpedo-shaped upper portion carrying the engine, steering gear and pilot, with the actual torpedo slung underneath. They were practically undetectable by Radar or Asdic. More than anything else they were a terror weapon.

This was not the last human torpedo contact the *Duff* would have. The Germans found them to be so successful that they pulled the E-boats out of the water and turned to the human torpedos to disrupt shipping in the English Channel and the *Duff* registered a number of 'kills'.

An insight into the crew's image of their Skipper is most notable in this quote from Griffiths' book, following a conversation between Brock and Lieutenant Commander Peter Scott.

I remember the Skipper and Peter Scott poring over the plot of the previous night's patrol, which had consisted of one futile chase after E-boats that had fled at full speed towards Cap d'Antifer. Lieutenant Commander Scott murmured as he followed the plot track: "Well, if they won't come out, the only thing left to do is to sail up the Seine and scare them out."

The Skipper grinned but those of us left in the Plot Room didn't. Fanciful as the idea seemed, it appeared less so when one recalled Peter Scott's reputation and when we knew how 'all for it' the Skipper was. The picture of the Duff sailing up the river, a few yards of water on either side, defying shore batteries and firing furiously into E-boat pens was, for a moment, a clear and frightening reality. Luckily, this suggestion stayed in the realms of the fanciful, but we had a feeling that the scene was becoming too quiet for the Skipper and that he would be trying soon to find a more active field.

The knowledge that there was something around that was looking for a target for its torpedoes, and that its presence was only advertised by the explosion of those torpedoes, was hardly likely to make anyone in those waters feel very secure.

The *Duff* had its share of close calls and, most memorably, a soul shattering experience where the entire crew saw their inevitable deaths bypassed through what many would call "a fluke."

They were lowering a motor boat to search for survivors of destroyer *Quorn* but there was a problem in the action and the boat jammed and veered towards the *Duff*. As a result the Skipper ordered a full stop of the engines until the problem could be resolved. As the Duff lost way a lookout shouted, "Torpedo track on port bow!"

"Get down!" the Skipper ordered.

"The bowchaser's crew watched petrified as the white track reached towards them, and looked down as it passed inches from the bows and disappeared into the night.

On the bridge everyone drew a deep breath, surprised to find themselves still alive.

"If we hadn't stopped," said an anonymous, wondering voice.

"Right under 'B' gun we'd have got it," came the answer.

The trancelike moment ended as an engine roared out and the motor boat curved off into the darkness.

"Half ahead both," came the order.

It wasn't until the *Duff* had returned to port that the Skipper made comment.

"The other night, on patrol, the motor boat was ordered away and, as you know, we had some trouble with the forward fall."

He stopped and looked at us for a few seconds.

"I know that incident probably saved the ship. But that doesn't matter. What does matter is the fact that

such a bloody bad piece of seamanship happened at all. I don't want it to occur again."

Wonderingly we looked at him as he stepped back and we pondered as the hymn cards were handed out. And as Lieutenant Bowles industriously pedalled the organ and our voices sang the hymn, we realised just how much of a captain the Skipper was. Luck can play a part in a ship's life, good luck or bad – but in the last analysis a ship's reputation, and indeed a ship's existence, depends mainly on the ship's company's seamanship. The Skipper realized this and made sure that we did, too.

It was time ...
for the Skipper to go home

Before the *Duff* was finally put to rest in some far off, American scrap heap, John Brock finally caught up with his brother after hearing that he was "mined" for the second time.

"John was very concerned," Evelyn Brock said. "He was delighted to find him looking well and sitting on the deck of the much damaged *Duff*, playing his mouth organ to a group of men.

"The two brothers were very close and great friends all of their lives. While Fred was assuring John that he was just great, a ship just entering port sounded it's siren ... and Fred jumped four feet off his chair!

"John said, 'I think you need some leave, Fred!'"

After the war Fred became a manufacturer's agent and determined to put the war behind him. He was quoted in an Evening Times-Globe article as saying,

"It's just one of those things that happened. And the kids today think it's terrible, so I just keep my mouth shut."

Unfortunately I was not able to access nearly as much information about John Brock, who also was awarded a DFC, also for sinking a U-boat which he accomplished while on duty in the Irish Sea. Like his brother, John was mentioned in numerous dispatches and was undoubtedly cut of the same heroic cloth.

He was in his fifth year of Royal Military College, Kingston, Ont. when war broke out. The class was graduated early in October, 1939 and, still in his cadetunifor, he left Halifax for the United Kingdom on a British battleship to take up a posting with *HMCS Assiniboine.*

The ship, which lacked a central heating system, was sent to Bermuda to chase German freighters before being refitted and put on fast convoy duty, to the *Clyde*, from Halifax. After two years with the *Assiniboine* John was made skipper of a minesweeper on convoy duty between Boston and Newfoundland and, six months later took over as skipper of the corvette *Badeque*, just 23 years old he was the youngest RCN officer to command a major war vessel.

The *Badeque* saw much action in the Mediterranean supporting the North Africa landings. The five Canadian corvettes in the group sank at least three submarines and downed a number of aircraft.

In 1945 he was given command of the new frigate *LaHulloise* (The Lady from Hull) at Montreal and was bringing her out of the St. Lawrence when the D-Day landings were announced. After a training cruise in Bermuda waters he took LaHulloise to convoy and patrol duty off the UK.

I have no doubt but that, had the action occurred in modern times, their sister, Eileen, an officer in the women's branch known as WRENS, would have acquitted herself equally as well as Fred and John. She was the youngest of the first class of 65 WRENS when the branch was formed. One of only two New Brunswickers in the group.

Eileen served in a number of responsible capacities in Vancouver, Ottawa, Halifax and Saint John from 1942 until her marriage in 1944.

The British Empire Medal

established August, 1917, amended 1922,
amended 1940, amended 1957

The British Empire Medal was introduced in 1917 as part of the *Order of the British Empire* for those who have rendered important services to the Empire. In 1918 a military division was created for all commissioned, warrant and subordinate officers of the military services.

In 1922 the medal was divided into the *Medal of the Most Excellent Order of the British Empire* for Gallantry (known as the *EGM–Empire Gallantry Medal*) and the *Medal of the Most Excellent Order of the British Empire*, for Meritorious Service (BEMM). The EGM was superseded by the *George Cross* in September 1940.

The BEM continued to be awarded for meritorious service after 1940 but also for gallantry.

(Please see page127 for full description)

Albert Hanley quietly went about his job ... saving St. John's Harbour from possible destruction

Here in the Western Hemisphere we tend to believe ourselves to be impervious to the vagaries of war. Oh, we know that we can be reached quickly and easily these days by space missiles and vehicles of all sorts, but it doesn't keep many of us awake nights!

So it was and has been over the past century or two. War raged far away on the other side of the Atlantic or the Pacific oceans but we went to bed at night and slept soundly, without fear of enemy intrusion. Oh yes, those of us who lived along Canada's coastlines knew that German submarines ... U-Boats as they were called ... slithered under the water here and there but that didn't keep us awake nights either.

If we are honest with ourselves we know that the truth is that we are surrounded by danger, wartime or not, but most of the time we never know about it. Which is just as well, really because most of the time there is precious little we could do about it anyway.

Fortunately, we also live in a world of every day heroes, quiet men and women who go about their jobs of protecting us.

The Navy, traditionally known as the "Silent Service" was very silent one day during the Second World War, turning to one of their most quiet branches, the naval deep sea divers, for a special assignment.

It was a risky operation.

A depth charge, laden with 350 lbs of TNT and two, loaded depth charge pistols had been lost off the stern of a warship into the harbour at St. John's, Newfoundland.

They had to be recovered.

As long as the TNT and the depth charge pistols remained at the bottom of the harbour they were a hazard, not only to the valuable warships lining the jetties but to the buildings and the street fronts beyond. Their explosion could set off a major catastrophe, reminiscent of the Halifax Explosion of 1917.

No one knew whether or not the depth charge was set to "safe". Up to a certain depth it would be impotent. But it was known that the two pistols were loaded with a highly explosive chemical. A slight jar was all that would be needed to detonate them and the chain reaction would set off the depth charge.

Fifty years ago deep sea divers were not the sleek frog-footed wraiths so popularized by television today. They were metal encumbered, lurching creatures in what looked and sounded like clanking space suits attached by a tenuous umbilical cord to an oxygen cylinder on the water's surface.

Imagine such a creature on the floor of a busy,

murky harbour, where the visibility was no more than seven feet at any one time, groping around trying to find these explosives and pistols. Then, once found, imagine the awkward creature's hands ensconced in bulky, thick-fingered gloves, attaching them securely to a dangling line ... all the time knowing that one wrong move would mean certain death followed by disaster.

When he learned that Able Seaman Albert J. Hanley of Saint John was the diver in line for the job the diving officer, Commissioner Bosun Lawrence "Lon" Chaney, felt a sense of relief.

"Just the man," he mused. "He's got to be cool and steady as a rock. This is going to be a tough job."

Hanley went over the side and, while his shipmates up top crossed their fingers, prayed and tended the life-line, he began to cruise the harbour bottom. An hour later he jerked his breast rope twice and the men breathed a sigh of relief.

They quickly hauled up the line and, dangling from it and attached by a precisely tied sailor's knot, was a dull metallic object not unlike a grease gun. They didn't have long to wait for the second signal. Fifteen minutes later they began hauling again, but this time the hoisting was harder and, as the line grew shorter, they could see the grey, cylindrical outline of the depth charge.

There was still one loaded depth charge pistol to be found. Time passed slowly both over and under the sea. Fifteen minutes, 45 minutes, an hour passed. This one was being elusive until suddenly there were two sharp tugs on the line. It was the sign the men were waiting for.

Hanley wanted them to hoist him up.

They hoisted. Up through the dirty, grey water of that wartime harbour came the second depth charge pistol, intact. Hanley's job was done.

He came to the surface, took off his helmet and said: "Now, boys–how about some lunch?"

A few short yards away the people of St. John's walked the streets of their city, heedless of the undersea drama which had saved their harbour and probably a few lives along the way.

Albert Hanley just considered this another day's work. But the people of Newfoundland did not think so.

At that time Newfoundland was not part of Canada, it was a British Colony so it bestowed the British Empire Medal on Able Seaman Hanley for his work that day.

Albert Hanley returned to Saint John when the war was over and eventually became property manager for the City of Saint John. He died in 1995, he was 77 years-old.

"He was a very laid-back kind of person, fun-loving, a good father and a good husband but he wasn't a pusher," said his widow Gertrude Hanley. She still lives in the home her husband built in the north end of the city nearly 50 years ago.

Author's Note: Mrs. Hanley supplied the material for this story from an article by Lieut. J.S. Keate of the RCNVR. Unfortunately there was no indication of what publication it appeared in, or when. A copy of the material also appeared in the Empire Digest vol. 2 no.4, January 1945. This material was simply signed Anonymous. **dd**

The Victoria Cross, the highest military award in the British Commonwealth

The Victoria Cross, awarded for the most conspicuous bravery or some daring or preeminent act of valour or self-sacrifice or extreme devotion to duty in the presence of the enemy.

The Victoria Cross is the British Commonwealth's highest military decoration for bravery. It was founded by Queen Victoria in 1856 to reward outstanding gallantry in the Crimean War.

The cross is a bronze cross patté, 1.375 inches across made from cannons captured from the Russians during the Crimean War.

The obverse displays the Royal Crown surmounted by a lion guardant. Below the crown a scroll, bears the inscription: *For Valour.*

The date of the act is engraved within a raised circle with raised edges on the reverse. It is suspended from a straight bar, ornamented with laurels and slotted for the ribbon, and has a v-lug below with a small link that joins it to a semicircular lug on the top of the cross. The ribbon was originally blue for the navy and red for the army but is now a dull crimson, regardless of which service the recipient represents.

The Victoria Cross is awarded, regardless of military rank, to members of the armed forces only.

Since 1972 the Cross of Valour, the Star of Courage and the Medal of Bravery represent Canada's highest decorations for bravery and may be awarded regardless of status to men or women either civilians or members of the armed forces.

The winners of the Victoria Cross had one thing in common, courage of the highest order. Defining courage is a difficult task. In the instance of the Victoria Cross, supporting evidence is thoroughly checked and eye witnesses are required before the cross can be awarded.

Three New Brunswickers have been awarded the Victoria Cross, all during the First World War. Their stories follow.

***

The Cross of Valour

Only one New Brunswicker has been awarded the Cross of Valour. It was a non-military occasion, the recipient was Anna Lang of Hampton, whose story may be found in the book *New Brunswick's Unsung Heroes*. *dd*

James Good singlehandedly emptied a German machine gun nest

On Aug. 8,1918 Canadian troops surprised the Germans by charging an 8,500 yard wide front, without warning the Germans ahead of time with the customary assault barrage. By nightfall the "shock troops" as the Germans had nicknamed the Canadians, with tank support, had advanced an unprecedented eight miles, captured 8,000 prisoners, 161 guns and countless rounds of ammunition at a cost of fewer than 4,000 casualties.

The action took place in the vicinity of Hangard Wood during the first day of the Canadian Corps attack in the Battle of Amiens. The troops, particularly Canadian troops, were moved back and forth from one location to another in order to confuse the Germans. They were particularly concerned with the Canadian troops since their presence anywhere spelled imminent attack both in the minds and in reality to the Germans.

It was the start of Canada's "100 Days" and it was the beginning of the end for Germany. That day four Canadians were awarded the Victoria Cross, only one of them survived: South Bathurst born Herman Good.

Herman James Good was born in South Bathurst on Nov. 29,1888. He was educated at Big River School and, after graduation, went into the lumber business in Gloucester County. In 1915, he went into the army and served with the 55th, 2nd Pioneer and 13th Battalions. After three years at the front, by the time the 1918 offensive was launched he had been wounded three times and held the rank of Corporal.

Aug. 8 was a day of drizzle fog and low cloud and the smoke from the artillery added more smoke to the atmosphere. The visibility was so bad the tanks were brought to a halt for fear of running over the infantry ahead of them and the troops behind the tanks were forced to hold up as well.

That was when the Germans began to fight back.

Good, with the 13th battalion, attacked a nest of three German machine guns that were holding up the regiment's advance.

With Herculean effort, he killed seven of the enemy crews and took the remainder prisoner. He then went on to a second exploit which he shared with three other Highlanders.

By late afternoon the regiment, which had been in the vanguard of the attack, had penetrated several miles into the enemy lines. Good and his men suddenly encountered an artillery battery of 5.9 inch cannon that was pinning down the Canadian advance and pounding positions to the rear.

At first glance, the idea of four men attacking the battery seemed out of the question ... they were badly outnumbered. But Good gambled that the enemy gunners would be inexperienced in hand-to-hand combat, the métier of the 13th Battalion.

Counting on the element of surprise he led a frontal assault that so unnerved the enemy artillery crews that they quickly surrendered and the Canadians captured three heavy enemy guns, without any losses.

Herman Good was presented with his Victoria Cross by King George V at Buckingham Palace on March 29, 1919. Shortly afterwards, he returned to the woods of New Brunswick and his home in Big River. He farmed and lumbered and served as fish, game and fire warden of the district for 20 years. In 1927 he joined the New Brunswick Travel Bureau and helped arrange provincial exhibits at sportsmen's shows in Boston and Philadelphia.

He was one of a select few taken to the White House in 1931 where, in full uniform, he presented President Herbert Hoover with a hamper of choice moose steaks, venison and Atlantic Salmon.

In 1962 he laid the cornerstone for the new Gloucester Branch of the Royal Canadian Legion and, in 1966, the new building was named after him and became "The Herman Good Branch."

He died in 1969 at 80 years of age and was buried in St. Alban's Cemetery. His son, Frank, who lives in Sudbury, Ontario, retained his father's Victoria Cross.

His Citation reads:

"Citation: For most conspicuous bravery and leading when, in attack, his company was held up by heavy fire from three enemy machine-guns, which were seriously delaying the advance. Realizing the gravity of the situation, this NCO dashed forward alone, killing several of the garrison and capturing the remainder. Later on Corporal Good, while alone, encountered a battery of 5.9 inch guns which were in action at the time. Collecting three men of his section, he charged the battery under point blank fire and captured the entire crews of the three guns." from the *London Gazette* of Sept 27, 1918.

Milton Fowler Gregg
'A Most Unlikely Hero'

The most unlikely hero one could imagine. An outstanding soldier who looked like someone's older uncle, yet won the nation's highest award for bravery. A far from accomplished speaker who could inspire the best in each of us. An indifferent administrator who built some of the most efficient organizations which served this nation. (Barney Danson, Canada's former Minister of National Defence)

On September of 1914, when the First World War broke out, Milton Gregg enlisted as a private in the 13th Canadian Infantry Battalion (Black Watch) and proceeded overseas. In 1915 he was wounded in battle and, the following year, took officer training, was commissioned and posted to the Royal Canadian Regiment.

At Lens in 1917 he led a bombing attack on a German machine-gun post using egg-shaped Mills bombs. Although wounded during the attack, he managed to carry a comrade to safety. He won the Military Cross for his bravery and courage, the first of many honours Milton Gregg was destined to receive in his lifetime.

In August of 1918 he added a Bar to the Military Cross (equivalent to a second Military Cross) at Monchy-le-Preux during an attack on the Bopis de Sart. In the teeth of devastating enemy fire he led a bombing party against two machine gun crews, killing them all. He later staved off a German counter attack.

In the same year he was awarded the VC at Cambrai. The citation reads:

"Citation: For most conspicuous bravery and initiative during the operations near Cambrai 27 Sept. to Oct 1, 1918; On Sept. 28, when the advance of the brigade was held up by fire from both flanks and by thick, uncut wire, Milton Gregg, a young school teacher from Kings County, crawled forward alone and explored the wire until he found a small gap, through which he subsequently led his men, and forced an entry into the enemy trench. The enemy counter-attacked in force and, through lack of bombs, the situation became critical. Although wounded Lt. Gregg returned alone under terrific fire and collected a further supply. Then, rejoining his party, which by this time was much reduced in numbers, and in spite of a second wound, he reorganized his men and led them with the greatest determination against the enemy trenches which he finally cleared.

"He personally killed or wounded 11 of the enemy and took 25 prisoners, in addition to 12 machine-guns captured in this trench. Remaining with his company, in spite of wounds, he again on Sept. 30, led his men in attack until severely wounded. The outstanding valour of this officer saved many casualties and enabled the advance to continue." London Gazette, Jan. 6, 1919.

Gregg recovered sufficiently from the wounds earned at Cambrai to return to his regiment, and to battle in time to join the November advance of Canadians that led to Mons.

Milton Fowler Gregg was born in Mountain Dale (near Sussex and known today as Snider Mountain), Kings County, New Brunswick on April 10, 1892. He was educated at the local school, the Provincial Normal School in Fredericton, Acadia and Dalhousie universities in Nova Scotia.

Prior to the First World War he taught school in New Brunswick and joined the local militia regiment, the 8th Hussars, in 1910.

During the Second World War he served with the Royal Canadian Regiment in England from December 1939 to April 1942. He was then promoted to colonel and sent to command the Officers' Training Corps at Brockville, Ont. In 1943 he became Brigadier and Commandant of the Canadian School of Infantry at Vernon, BC a post he held until the end of the war.

Following the war he served for several years as President of the University of New Brunswick, until answering a call to the federal Cabinet, where he was successively Minister of Fisheries, Minister of Veterans' Affairs then Minister of Labour until1956. He maintained residences in both Fredericton and Ottawa and continued to enjoy a long and consistently prestigious career.

Much of his time was spent working with the United Nations in Iraq and Indonesia as Canadian Representative to the United Nations. In 1964, at 71 years of age, he became Canada's High Commissioner to Guyana.

Three years later he retired, officially, to Fredericton but continued his active lifestyle until his death on March 31, 1978. Following the funeral service at Christ Church Cathedral in Fredericton he was buried in the Snider Mountain Baptist Cemetery.

A sad postscript to this story is that Milton Gregg's well-earned Victoria Cross was stolen on Christmas Eve, 1978 from the RCR Museum in London, Ontario. It has never been recovered.

Cyrus Peck cited for Conspicuous Bravery

Cyrus Peck won his first medal, the Distinguished Service Order, in April, 1917 during the Canadian attack on Vimy Ridge.

On Sept. 2, 1918 his regiment's advance was blocked by the Germans at Villers-lez-Cagnicourt. A Lieutenant-Colonel at the time, he nevertheless personally reconnoitred the area ahead of his troops in the face of relentless machine-gun and sniper fire. After assessing the situation he returned to his headquarters, reorganized the battalion so that both flanks were properly covered, and charged forward at the head of his men. Travelling under intense artillery shelling he sought out the tank corps and, drawing on the knowledge he had gathered in reconnoitring the German positions, he was able to direct the tanks to fresh objectives. The tanks then overcame the enemy resistance and paved the way for a Canadian infantry battalion to move forward, with the support of his own battalion.

His citation reads as follows:

Citation: "For most conspicuous bravery and skilful leading when in attack under intense fire. His command quickly captured the first objective, but progress to the further objective was held up by enemy machine-gun fire on his right flank.

"The situation being critical in the extreme, Col.

Peck pushed forward and made a personal reconnaissance under heavy machine gun and sniping fire, across a stretch of ground which was heavily swept by fire ...

"... His magnificent display of courage and fine qualities of leadership enabled the advance to be continued, although always under heavy artillery and machine-gun fire, and contributed largely to the success of the brigade attack." *London Gazette*, Nov. 15, 1918.

A month later Peck was wounded, ending a distinguished combat career.

Cyrus Wesley Peck was born at Hopewell Hill, April 26, 1871. He was educated in Hopewell Hill schools until he was 16 years old and his family moved to New Westminster, BC (sources vary as to the date he left New Brunswick).

He later went to Skeena, BC becoming a broker and general agent in salmon canning, sawmill and towing operations then joined the militia in 1900, but was refused for the Boer War.

After the First World War started Peck joined the 30th Battalion on Nov. 1, 1914 and was given a Captain's commission. In February of 1915 he sailed for England and in April he was promoted to Major and transferred to the 167th Battalion and proceeded to France. On May 15 he was wounded in both legs but by January of 1916 he was given command of his regiment with the rank of Lieut. Colonel, which rank he held when awarded the Victoria Cross at Villers-lez-Cagnicourt on Sept. 2, 1918.

Cyrus Peck was an outstanding figure on the home front as well. He actually became involved in politics even before his career in the military. He was the Member of Parliament for Skeena, B.C. and had the distinction of being the first Canadian re-elected to Parliament in absentia.

He is also credited with reintroducing the playing of the bagpipes on the battlefield.

Peck continued his career in politics on returning to British Columbia and took a strong interest in veterans' rights and also commanded the Canadian Bisley rifle team. He died at his home "Hopewell," named for his Albert County birthplace, on Sept. 27, 1976 just after returning from the Victoria Cross Centenary celebrations in England.

His medal is now with the national collection at the National War Museum in Ottawa.

The story of an 'ordinary' soldier

John T. McDermott has to be one of the most determined soldiers to ever serve Canada on a volunteer basis. He was so determined, in fact, that he managed to serve in three different wars over a span of thirty years, from 1884 until 1915.

McDermott was a member of the local militia in Saint John but, whenever there was an opportunity for active duty, he would be among the first in line. On each occasion, for some unknown reason, he also lied about his age .

One day, in the course of his research into all things military, historian Byron O'Leary of Saint John came across some of McDermott's medals, all of which were inscribed with his name. O'Leary was curious about this man and proceeded to research his military career.

"By studying the careers of individual soldiers, like McDermott, the military historian is better able to understand his subject and to keep things in their proper perspective," O'Leary says.

Studying about McDermott led O'Leary into an area frequently ignored by historians.

"The field of military biography is devoted almost entirely to the study of those of commissioned rank. This is, in part, due to their high visibility and to the fact that career information on officers is more readily available than is similar information on other ranks.

"While it is true that officers do, through their leadership role, exert a disproportionate amount of influence upon the units with which they serve, it must also be remembered that they form less than ten per cent of the effective strength of their units.

"Even the best of officers could do little without the other ranks to carry out their orders. The few 'other ranks' biographies which have been written are almost entirely devoted to men who have been decorated, such as Victoria Cross, Medal of Honour winners and the like.

"Such biographies certainly make interesting reading but they do not rectify the bias, in military biography, towards the commissioned ranks."

O'Leary subsequently wrote the biography of John McDermott and it was published in the Summer, 1989 issue of *Canadian Military Biography*.

"It is," he says, "a step towards the creation of a body of such 'other ranks' biographies."

A meticulous historian, O'Leary traced McDermott's story through a myriad of sources including burial records, the *Canada Gazette*, the *1881 Census*, newspaper accounts in the *Saint John Daily Sun*, *Daily Telegraph*, *Evening Times Globe*, the *New Freeman*, *The Saint John Globe*, *Saint John Star* and the *Saint John Weekly Freeman*. In addition he sought material in numerous books, magazines and military files. The depth of this research is apparent in his chronicling of McDermott's fascinating, and at times amusing, military career.

Byron O'Leary has been kind enough to let me take liberties with his biography and present the following, limited, account of a most unusual and sincere soldier of another era.

John T. McDermott... a dedicated volunteer soldier in three wars

John T. McDermott was the first member of his family to be born in what is now Canada, in Saint John, New Brunswick on July 6, 1864.

Although the family was not well-to-do he had some schooling and learned a trade, that of an "Iron Moulder" and contributed regularly to the support of his mother and younger sisters.

In June of 1884, at the age of 19, he joined the *Sixty Second "Saint John Fusiliers" Battalion* of the volunteer militia (commonly referred to as the *Saint John Fusiliers*).

On March 26,1885 the Northwest Rebellion began and when his commanding officer, Lieutenant Colonel Arbuthnot Blaine, put out a call for volunteers John T. McDermott was right there. On May 18 he left by train for Sussex to become a part of the *New Brunswick Provisional Battalion*, later the *NB&PEI Provincial Battalion*.

Alas, all his training and volunteering came to naught. Louis Riel was captured on May 15, the Metis and Indian resistance collapsed and his battalion's services were not required.

So much for War Number One.

By July, 1890 McDermott had been promoted in the militia to the rank of corporal, then to the rank of Sergeant in 1891. Unfortunately a month later he was demoted to private again. It would appear the demotion was not a demerit and O'Leary suspects it came about because McDermott preferred to stay with the Saint John Fusiliers where, in 1892, he was presented with three, long service and good conduct chevrons.

By now the Boer War was heating up and, on October 13, 1899, the Canadian government offered the British War Office a contingent of one thousand infantrymen. John T. McDermott was right there at the front of the line, ready to go.

Recruiting began on October 19. By the following evening he was volunteering for service in South Africa. At this time he was actually 35 years old but, when recruited, he gave his age as 32. On October 30 he sailed for Africa on the *Sardinian*, arriving in Capetown on November 29 ... only to be left behind as part of a small party designated to tend the battalion's store.

Undaunted Private McDermott eventually left Capetown with four other members of his company and they rejoined their regiment at Belmont in the Orange Free State on January 16, 1900. Here they performed garrison duties on the railway lines until mid-February. They were then moved forward to join the Nineteenth Brigade in the pursuit of General Piet Cronje and his troops.

General Cronje made his stand at Paardeberg Drift on February 18. McDermott took part in what was to be an ill-fated charge, emerging unscathed nevertheless from his first baptism by fire.

The Boers withdrew up river that night and McDermott's regiment also moved three miles up river then, on the morning of February 20, moved forward to within approximately one thousand yards of the nearest Boer defences.

McDermott, on sentry duty, began to suffer from cramps. He was subsequently relieved of duty and sent, alone, to the New South Wales Field Hospital, located about three miles downstream.

In his misery McDermott trudged down-stream to a pontoon ferry where he crossed the Modder River and started following the wagon ruts which passed for roads in that part of Africa. He followed the road until it intersected with the road to Bloemfontein and turned west to continue down stream towards the hospital. At this point it is believed that McDermott either passed the hospital in the dark or simply overestimated the distance he had travelled. In either case he decided to turn back and return to his own lines.

But McDermott missed the turn at the intersection and continued up the Bloemfontein Road instead.

His first indication of trouble came when the Boer pickets opened fire on him. He went to ground but, before he could withdraw, was surrounded by a dozen armed Boers who called for him to surrender.

Which he did.

In doing so he earned the dubious distinction of being the first Canadian to become a prisoner of war during the Anglo-Boer War of 1899-1902.

Both General Conje and his personal secretary questioned him but McDermott, now in the throes of full-blown dysentery, offered no information. The secretary recommended he be shot as, in his opinion, "All Colonials should be shot as they had no business being in South Africa."

The general was less bloodthirsty and sent McDermott to the prisoners' compound. The prisoners had dug themselves a shelter located between the Boers' ammunition wagons and the river. McDermott maintained the prisoners were well treated, despite the shortage of rations being experienced by the Boers.

On February 27 McDermott's regiment decided to advance on General Conje's encampment in the pre-dawn hours, in an attempt to force the Boers to surrender. The advance was a success and the Boers piled their weapons in the ammunition area before leaving their positions to surrender. McDermott and the other prisoners then picked up weapons and stood guard over the surrendered arms until the Canadians moved forward and occupied the area.

Later that afternoon, after congratulating the regiment on the work they had done, Lord Roberts stopped and spoke with none other than Private John T. McDermott. Before leaving, Roberts told the adjutant to make certain that McDermott, who by now was considerably emaciated, received medical attention right away.

Nevertheless McDermott stayed in the field with the regiment. No doubt he did not want to wander astray and into enemy hands again, no matter how well the Boers had treated him!

In March he took part in the action at Driefontein but a few weeks later he was hospitalized with enteric fever and, by the end of May he had been sent to England to recover.

By September he was on his way home to Canada.

From the time McDermott and other veterans arrived on the Canadian shores at Quebec they were fêted at receptions and wined and dined. When he and four other New Brunswick soldiers arrived in Saint John they were treated to a civic reception and a luncheon at the prestigious *Union Club.*

Later that day McDermott was officially discharged, despite having been considered as yet unfit to resume his civilian occupation.

A number of social functions for the returning veterans ensued, including a Soldiers' Banquet at the St. Andrew's Rink and a ceremony at the Sons of England Hall, where he was presented with a gold watch.

The final fête occurred on October 17, 1901.

In the morning the returned soldiers, who lived in the Saint John area, paraded at the City's Court House. Each was presented with a scroll, awarding them the rights and privileges of a Freeman of the City of Saint John.

The scrolls were presented in leather tubes which bore the City's crest and the individual's name in gilt.

The same afternoon His Royal Highness, the Duke of Cornwall and York (later to be crowned King George V) presented one hundred and thirty-one Queen's South Africa medals to returned soldiers from both New Brunswick and Prince Edward Island.

McDermott eventually received three clasps to go with his medal, one each representing the battles at Cape Colony, Paardeberg and Driefontein.

The same war, another call

On November 29, 1901, the Canadian government was again recruiting for service in South Africa. McDermott, of course, was right there. He passed his medical just fine but O'Leary has not yet found the record so it is difficult to say what age he gave on this occasion. What he didn't pass was his riding skills test. O'Leary suggests that he may never have ridden a horse before, although at the time the horse was the primary mode of travel.

Again, in March of 1902, more mounted troops were called for and, once more, John T. McDermott applied to enlist, giving his age as thirty-four although, in truth, he was thirty-seven years old by then.

Nevertheless, by May 8, 1902 McDermott was on board the S.S. *Cestrian* as it sailed out of Halifax and eventually found himself at the Port of Durban in Natal. Now, obviously reasonably skilled in horsemanship, he and his mount moved inland to Fort Hay where they stayed until receiving their orders to return to Canada.

The Peace of Vereeniging was signed on May 31,1902 making McDermott and the others "redundant."

Once more his return to Saint John was marked by social engagements and, in late 1904, he was awarded the Colonial Auxiliary Forces Long Service Medal in recognition of 20 years with the Canadian Militia.

On June 26, 1905 he re-enlisted in the militia.

Another war, another challenge

On August 4, 1914 Great Britain entered the growing conflict in Europe and, once again, Canada was at war and, once again, on August 30 to be exact, John T. McDermott enlisted for active service and was accepted. This time he gave his age as forty-two when, in reality, he was now fifty years-old.

During morning drill on September 18 the members of McDermott's company were asked to volunteer for overseas or foreign service. The following account appeared in a local newspaper as a result.

All the officers and men of the company of the 62nd Regiment, St. John Fusiliers doing duty as regular troops during yesterday morning's drill volunteered for foreign service. When the company was asked there was only one hesitant and that was because the man knew he was suffering from varicose veins and he hesitated from a fear of not passing the doctor. On it being explained to him the fact might not be a disqualification he also stepped out and so, with perfect unanimity, the whole company of fifty-nine volunteered. (The Daily Telegraph, September 19,1914.)

O'Leary writes, *Whether or not McDermott was the one man who hesitated we shall probably never know.*

But McDermott's luck finally ran out. It was discovered that a number of troops were not medically fit for active duty. Stricter medical examinations were ordered,McDermott was declared medically unfit.

Although it was the end of his military career it was not the end of his war effort. By late 1916 he was working at McAvity and Sons Limited where he manufactured artillery shells until the end of the war.

The Depression took its toll on this soldier, work was hard for him to find and his health was failing. In late 1935, at the age of seventy, he retired and was granted a military pension on the basis of his service in South Africa. He died at home at the age of seventy-six.

"Of equal importance to his military service was his life as a productive member of society," O'Leary says.

In total, although he volunteered for active service on five separate occasions and in three wars, in reality John T. McDermott crowded a whole other lifetime into only two years of active military service.

The Military McLeans
served the nation well

In the course of researching material for this book on New Brunswick wartime stories I kept coming across the name "McLean" and began to wonder about the co-incidence of the number of McLeans with distinguished military careers. Was I encountering the same person every time? I wondered.

Eventually I realized that two of them were actually father and son but the third was a separate entity. Related? Perhaps, but I decided my genealogical research had gone far enough for the purposes of this book.

Each of these men was outstanding in serving his country and assuming leadership roles both militarily and throughout their auspicious peacetime careers. They are indeed New Brunswickers of whom we can be proud.

Hugh H. McLean, Brigadier-General and Lieutenant Governor

This McLean saga starts with Hugh Havelock McLean who was born in Fredericton in 1854. He started out his mature life as a certified surveyor, later moving on to study law and be admitted to the bar in 1875. On his eightieth birthday it was noted that he was the oldest practising lawyer in New Brunswick.

He was made Lieutenant-Governor of New Brunswick in 1928, at the age of seventy-four and enjoyed his eightieth birthday in that capacity before retiring around 1933 or 1934.

However, it is Hugh H. McLean's military life that I find most intriguing. I was fascinated with the number of instances where crowned heads and government personages thanked him profusely for his military activity ... yet he had no particular military medals to show for it. Although I suppose the title of "Major General" was a military honour and becoming Lieutenant Governor was a form of political honour.

What intrigued me about this man was that, every time I turned a page of research, I found him raising an army for a variety of reasons ... all at his own expense.

His obituary referred to his being an "ardently patriotic man."

A masterpiece of understatement!

H.H. McLean began his military career fighting the Fenians. It was just before Confederation and there were those who were certain that an American branch of the Irish Fenian Society was on its way to attack New Brunswick. Then there are those who, to this day, maintain it was a federalist Tory ploy which succeeded in bringing New Brunswick on side on the issue of Confederation.

No matter, H.H. McLean went forth and looked for Fenians, ready to fight them if need be to save his country for Great Britain.

A few years later, in 1878, when war between Russia and England was "imminent," at his own expense he raised a company of men ready to fight for England in that war.

Again, in 1885, he was appointed Captain and Adjutant of the New Brunswick and Prince Edward Island Regiment fitting them out and training them for battle in the Northwest Rebellion. Later, in 1889, he went to England in command of Canada's Bisley team.

But wars and threat of wars continued as the Victoria Empire blossomed and in 1899 McLean offered to raise 100 men for service in what is commonly called the Boer War in South Africa. By 1901 he commanded all the troops in New Brunswick which were assembled in Saint John during the Royal Visit of the Duke and Duchess of Cornwall and York.

There were a few years of respite from war before the First World War erupted in 1914. In those intervening years he became active in politics and was first elected to Parliament as a *Liberal* in 1908 then re-elected in 1917 under the *Unionist* banner.

But by 1917 there was apparently a need for more troops and, once again, into the breech moved Brigadier General H.H. McLean, now in command of the 7th Infantry Brigade to assist once more in raising troops, this time the 236th Battalion CEF, which became known as the *McLean Highlanders.*

If members of the "Boomer" generation of the 20th Century are labelled "Over Achievers" one can only imagine what label might be applied today to a man such as Hugh Havelock McLean.

Little wonder that his son, Charles Wesley Weldon McLean, was an outstanding soldier and parliamentarian in his lifetime as well.

Distinguished Service Order

Royal Warrant published in London Gazette
November 9, 1886

Terms: The order was established for rewarding individual instances of meritorious or distinguished service in war. This is a military order for officers only, and while normally given for service under fire or under conditions equivalent to service in actual combat with the enemy, it was awarded between 1914 and 1916 under circumstances which could not be regarded as under fire. After January 1, 1917, commanders in the field were instructed to recommend this award only for those serving under fire. Prior to 1943, the order could be given only to someone "Mentioned-in-Dispatches." The order is generally given to officers in command, above the rank of Lieutenant-Colonel and awards to ranks below this are usually for a high degree of gallantry just short of deserving the Victoria Cross.

Bars: A bar is awarded for an act which would have earned the order in the first place. The bar is plain gold with an Imperial Crown in the centre. The year of the award is engraved on the reverse.

Description: A gold cross, enamelled gold and edged in gold.

Obverse: In the centre, within a wreath of laurel,

enamelled green, the Imperial Crown in gold upon a red enamelled ground.

<u>Reverse:</u> Within a wreath of laurel, enamelled green, the Royal Cypher in gold upon a red enamelled ground. A ring at the top of the medal attaches to a ring at the bottom of a gold bar, ornamented with laurel. At the top of the ribbon is a second gold bar ornamented with laurel.

<u>Ribbon</u>: The red ribbon is 1.125 inches wide with narrow blue edges. A rosette is worn on the ribbon in undress to signify the award of a bar.

Although officially names are not inscribed on the cross, some recipients have privately had their names engraved on the back of the suspension bar.

Charles Wesley Weldon McLean earned the DSO and two Bars

Charles Wesley Weldon McLean was born in Saint John on Aug. 26, 1882. He was the son of a distinguished military father, Major-General Hugh Havelock McLean, a King's Counsel and Member of Parliament, and Jennie M. (Porteous) McLean.

The younger McLean studied at the Royal Military College in Kingston and, on March,7 1900 at the age of 18, entered the Royal Artillery as a Second Lieutenant in time to take part in the South African – better known as the "Boer" - War. He participated in the advance on Kimberley, was present at operations at Orange Free State, including Paardeberg, and saw action at Poplar Grove and Dreifontein and at Cape Colony, south of Orange River, for which actions he was awarded the Queen's Medal with three clasps.

Young McLean was a career soldier and advanced rapidly in rank becoming a Major by the time the First World War started in 1914.

On Sept. 21, 1915, while serving with the 52nd Brigade, Royal Field Artillery, Major McLean's observation station was hit. Although he was stunned as a result of the attack he remained at his post and continued to oversee the fire of his guns until, on Sept. 25, "with great dash" (according to his citation) he was able to bring his battery forward over the open and provide close support to the infantry near Hohenzollern Redoubt.

Still under heavy fire, Major McLean immediately ran a communications wire to the battalion headquarters. He then continued to observe the battalion's fire from a very exposed position until after dark. He was wounded after rejoining his battery but refused to leave until he had brought his command out of action.

For these actions, other acts of conspicuous gallantry and his ability to accomplish difficult yet vital tasks, demonstrated on many occasions during May and September of 1915, he was awarded the Distinguished Service Order with two Bars.

A Canadian Press story on Friday, July 20, 1917 noted that McLean received a second Bar to the Distinguished Service Order, according to the official *Gazette* of July 18. The story said that ... "Twice on the same day Major McLean went forward at great personal risk into a heavy barrage fire to reconnoitre. The following day he led a party under heavy shell fire to extinguish a fire which threatened to cause grave casualties, and succeeded in saving guns and munitions.

Now "Colonel" McLean went to England after the war and became a Member of Parliament for Brig. He died on Sept. 5, 1962.

Charles Herbert McLean, DSO career soldier, lawyer and publisher

Lieut.-Col. Charles Herbert McLean was born in Saint John on May 16, 1877, the son of Lauchlan and Sofia LeBrun Duplissie (Marsh) McLean. He served in the Spanish-American War with the 1st Ohio Cavalry and was appointed a Lieutenant with the 8th Princess Louise's (N.B.) Hussars in March of 1909.

He became a Major with the 28th N.B. Dragoons in March of 1911. McLean originated, and was named Major in Command of, "B" Squadron with the 6th Canadian Mounted Rifles, sailing for England in July of 1915. He was in France by October and he and the "B" Squadron were transferred to the 4th CMR and McLean was appointed commander of "D" company. He served in France from October until the Armistice and was promoted to the rank Of Lieutenant-Colonel while in France.

Lt. Col. McLean was twice mentioned in despatches and received the Distinguished Service Order "for conspicuous gallantry and devotion to duty near Valenciennes, Nov. 1, 1918.

"With a view to locating points for bridging the Escant Canal he and one man crossed it on an improvised bridge of plank, a raft and a boat.

"Once across, McLean was immediately under fire from a machine gun, which he promptly attacked, killing one man and holding the remainder at bay until assistance arrived. He then captured the machine gun and ten men. As a result a Post was established enabling a crossing of the entire battalion frontage without a casualty."

When he returned from overseas Col. McLean took over command of the New Brunswick Dragoons and was ADC to then Lieutenant-Governor McLean during his term of office from 1928-1933.

Although educated toward a legal career McLean chose a career first as an Information Officer then as a publisher. He was president of the McLean Agency, with offices in Albany, N.Y. and Hamilton, Ont. He was also secretary-treasurer of Smith Publishing Company in Toronto, embracing 12 weekly papers. Among the books he published was *Prominent People of New Brunswick*, in 1937 ... from which the foregoing material on him was gleaned.

The Military Cross
established December 28, 1915

Terms: The Military Cross can be awarded to commissioned officers of the substantive rank of Captain or below (therefore acting and temporary Majors are eligible) or Warrant Officers for distinguished and meritorious services in battle. In 1920, the terms were altered to clearly state the award was for gallant and distinguished services in action and that naval and air force officers could be awarded the cross for gallant and distinguished services on the ground.

Description: A plain silver cross, 1.75 inches across.

Obverse: On each arm of the cross is an Imperial Crown and in the centre of the cross is the Imperial and Royal Cypher of the reigning sovereign (GV, GVI, or EIIR).

Reverse: The reverse is plain with the year of the award engraved on the lower arm.

Mounting: The ring welded to the top of the cross is joined to the plain straight suspender ring by a small ring (three rings). A watered white ribbon (1.375 inches wide), with a central purple stripe (0.5 inches).

Don Smith, MC and Bar
one of Carleton & York's finest

Some day, if I live long enough, I may do a book about growing up on Olive Street. It's a little street in West Saint John, just a bare block long but packed full of history for all that.

I lived there in the "Dirty Thirties" from the time I was around five until I was about 12 years old. Whether it was the times or the people that made it so special I don't know, probably a bit of both ensured that Olive Street's impression on me was a lasting one. Three of my personal heroes lived on Olive Street, I adored them then and I still do.

They were the big brothers I yearned for and I adopted them for eternity, whether they liked it or not, and "not" was more frequently the case I am sure. Who needs a kid, a girl at that, 10 years or more younger dogging your footsteps all the time?

Bill and Don Smith were the sons of Mamie and Ted Smith, our neighbours and friends to one side, and "Wink" (Winston) Johnson was the son of "Doc" Johnson our landlord and neighbour on the other side. I often suspected that Wink was not impressed when I also adopted his dog, Jiggs, but that's another story.

All three of my big brothers "joined up" early in the Second World War, eager to fight for their country. All three went into the *Carleton & York Regiment* and managed to see a lot of action.

Wink was the oldest and reached the rank of Major quickly. Wink is also the one of the three who did not come back. He was in Italy in December, 1943, commanding 'A' Company during the battle for *Ortona.*

"The First Canadian Division's plan for the capture of Ortona fell into four phases: first, the establishment of a bridgehead over the Moro River: second, clearing the gully parallel to, and south of, the Ortona-Orsogna lateral: third the capture of Ortona itself: fourth an encircling movement north of Ortona to drive off the remaining Germans ...

"The enemy was carrying out a systematic demolition of all road bridges on our line of advance ... construction of Bailey bridges was a major limiting factor in our rate of advance ... The winter rains had commenced. The ground was soft and difficult off the roads and tracks for the cross-country movement of both men and vehicles." (*Invicta. The Carleton and York Regiment in the Second World War* by Robert Tooley.)

The *Carleton & York Regiment* would be involved in the second and fourth phases. Militarily it was difficult country for the offensive. First Canadian Division's line of advance was at right angles to a series of rivers, deep valleys and steep gullies running down to the Adriatic. They were to clear the gully with an encircling movement north of Ortona.

During the first phase of the Ortona battle, *Three Canadian Infantry Brigade* remained in reserve and the *Carleton & York* acted as the Brigade's advance guard with 'A' Company, commanded by Major W.C. Johnson (Wink) in the vanguard.

According to Tooley's account, the journey was slow owing to rain, the slippery roads, the heavy traffic at the bridge and vehicles attempting to pass the convoy. There was concern at Brigade Headquarters about the bad effect on morale of what it considered excessive and ill-advised gossip about casualties.

On Dec. 13 the *Carleton and York* attacked at 6 a.m. with 'A' company and 'D' company leading the way, one on each side of the main axis. Things went well at first but the Artillery barrage didn't neutralize the enemy and they eventually lashed the Carleton and York companies with a hail of machine gun and small arms fire as they showed their heads above the gully.

Undaunted, the Carleton and York launched another attack but could make little progress against the murderous machine gun, mortar and artillery fire on a scale the brigade had never experienced before. Nevertheless, they managed to inflict heavy casualties on the enemy and took 21 prisoners but the battalion suffered severe losses and was badly shaken.

On Dec. 20 the consensus at a Brigade conference was that "it was impossible for a frontal attack to be successful ..." with the proviso that two battalions with great concentrations of smoke might have succeeded.

Nevertheless, on Dec. 23 the fourth phase of the Ortona operation began. A false intelligence report indicated that the Germans had withdrawn behind the Foro River, two miles beyond Arielli. Subsequently on Dec. 31, 1943, 'A' and 'D' companies set out again, this time for Point 59.

Unfortunately it wasn't until noon hour that the inaccuracies in the intelligence report were revealed, by then the two companies had once more come under heavy fire from artillery, mortars and machine guns. Although they were within 600 yards of their target the

fire was unexpectedly heavy and the losses were devastating, among them the Commander of 'A' Company,
Major Winston "Wink" Johnson.

Wink didn't get any medals for his battles but
the story I was told, as a kid, was that when Don Smith
heard of Wink's death he was enraged and the adrenaline flowed faster and continued to flow at a fast pace
until, on January 4, he struck back with a vengeance.

Like Wink, Don was also at Ortona, a Lieutenant
in 'B' company at the time. That day 'B', 'C' and 'D'
companies crossed the start line at four o'clock in the
afternoon, after a day-long artillery attack. Their target ... Point 59.

The Germans launched a combined infantry and
tank attack but their initiative was cut short by Lieut.
Don Smith. As the officer commanding #11 Platoon,
'B' company Smith, supported by #12 Platoon under
Lieut. C.R. Segee, seized the tower ... "doing wonders
for the *Carleton and York Regiment's* morale".

Lieut. Smith's Platoon was given the credit for
"routing a company of paratroops" and Don Smith had
earned his first Military Cross.

.   Later, in December of that year, another "West
Sider," Lieut. Rod Logan, a member of D company under the command of now *Capt.* Don Smith MC, relates
how he watched "Don and three other guys pushing a
six pounder, an anti-tank gun ... they were literally
manhandling the thing. I don't know to this day how it
got there or where it came from; whether it was one of
ours ... or if it belonged to the Germans ... but they
were determined to get it into position. And they did
too."

According to Tooley the Germans had launched an attack with infantry, two Panthers and a Tiger (tanks) down the road to the canals. This threatening development was cut short by the initiative of Capt. Smith along with Capt. P.G. Newell, Sergeants Jimmy Agnew and Dick Peterson hauling a six-pounder anti-tank gun over the canal and across fields to 'D' Company's left hand platoon.

"They then aimed the six pounder at the leading Panther tank and pumped several shells into it, successfully knocking it out and blocking the road to further advance by the other two tanks, which quickly retired to cover. Capt. Newell then called down the artillery while Smith returned to 'C' company and shot up the Germans."

Both officers were awarded bars to go with the Military Crosses they had already earned by this time.

The battle for Ortona will continue to be fought in the history books and military buffs will continue to argue over where to lay the blame for an ill-fought battle until all living memory of the event is past.

By April 24 of 1945 now 'Major' Don Smith, MC and Bar was leading 'D' Company in their last battle only to be wounded twice, the second time by an S mine on the *Carleton & York Regiment's* last day of fighting. A local truce for the Canadian Corps was declared on April 28.

Don Smith lost a leg and most of the sight of one eye on that final day. He returned home to university and ultimately to add the initials M.D. (Doctor of Medicine) to the hero's honours so bravely won. He moved to Oshawa, Ontario in the late 1950s where he practised as an internist until his retirement.

Don's older brother, Bill, was wounded while fighting in Africa with the British and returned to England.

"I was never able to get back up to snuff again," he told me, "and had to do what I could behind the scenes."

Bill later went on to become a Rhodes Scholar and retired as Dean of Economics at the University of New Brunswick.

The Three Jacks

Will R. Bird wrote a book called *The Two Jacks* back in 1960 and I remember being fascinated with the story at the time. I reread it recently and found it had held up well over the years and I was delighted to learn, when talking to one of those Jacks that it may soon be reprinted.

Great news!

While it is available through the Regional Library system original copies are getting more and more time-worn and scarce.

In the meantime I am pleased to include some excerpts from the adventures of those two Jacks as part of this story of *The Three Jacks*.

And who are these Three Jacks?

Two of them are named Jack Fairweather, father and son, Rothesay natives, and the third is Jack Veness of Fredericton.

The first of the 'Jacks'

The senior Jack Fairweather was born in 1878, served in the First World War as a Lieutenant and later a Captain with #4 O/S Battery. During April 10, 11 and 12, 1917, his actions resulted in his being awarded the Military Cross.

As Forward Observation Officer (F.O.O.) at Bur Trench Fairweather was required to go ahead of the troops as a scout, to determine as much information as possible concerning enemy deployment and strength.

Byron O'Leary told me Fairweather would also be required to send information concerning the distances to which the artillery should be targeted back to the lines. The artillery would then fire an exploratory round at his direction, following which he would advise them of what adjustments would be needed prior to an all out attack.

On April 12, Lieut. Fairweather went forward with a party to extend the telephone lines and establish an O.P. (Observation Post). He wrote the following vivid description of the field after the battle:

It had snowed during the night and a cold wind was blowing. The state of the country we went over is almost beyond description; simply a waste with no distinguishing marks. Shell hole upon shell hole, some big enough to put a small house in, and most filled with water and mud. A tangled mass of old wire, iron, equip-

ment, and, here and there, the bodies of friend and foe, a ghastly sight.

The observation post in Bur Trench was of yeoman service throughout the day, not only to the 4th Battery, but to the neighbouring 72nd. Siege, (South Africa) and to numbers 131 and 272.

On June 9, 1917 he was awarded the Military Cross for "excellent work and devotion to duty while acting as F.O.O. His citation read:

Having established his observation post in an advanced position, he displayed great coolness and courage under heavy fire. His services were most invaluable on this occasion, as he was able to register three batteries on an enemy position with most satisfactory results.

Educated as a lawyer, with a degree from Harvard, Capt. Fairweather returned to Rothesay after the war and entered politics. He was elected to the New Brunswick Legislature in 1930 and was appointed a Judge of the Supreme Court of New Brunswick in 1935.

And *The Two Jacks*

On *D-Day*, June 6, 1944, Jack Fairweather waded ashore at Dieppe, France to the skirl of bagpipes through water that was chin-deep. He didn't notice the water, all he saw and heard were the smoke, the bagpipes and the guns of battle.

His adrenaline was flowing at full tilt.

When the smoke cleared they discovered they had been piped right into Berniére-sur Mer. He marvelled that the town and the total environment were exactly as he had been shown during training in England.

The troops had been trained well. They may not have known where they had landed but they knew every yard of road and field.

But as luck would have it Fairweather's regiment, the North Novas, had gone through a break in the seawall directly into town ... only to discover that they had arrived before the advance brigade!

The troops that were supposed to be in front of them – were behind them!

As a result they lost two hours, then discovered their platoon had turned the wrong way at a fork in the road. When the mistake was realized the platoon was

turned around and Jack Veness ended up leading them back the way they had come only to find themselves in the midst of a vicious battle.

It was a massacre that would give them nightmares for years to come. The few troops still alive were surrounded, prisoners of machine-gun wielding Hitler Youth troops.

Thus began the long march that would see the two Jacks team up in what was to be the adventure of their lives.

Columns of prisoners, guarded by German tanks and troops proceeded eastward on their five-day, one hundred and thirty-five mile trek. Within the first three hours the column of prisoners was attacked four times by allied planes that roared down from the sky, guns blazing , attempting to blast to eternity what to them appeared to be German troops.

The final attack on the first day came when eight American *Lightenings* zoomed down from nowhere, "buzzing around like hornets disturbed in a hayfield, shooting from all angles, swooping down to one hundred feet and firing short bursts, then turning and doing it all again."

In truth, outside of sore feet and empty stomachs, the greatest danger the prisoners experienced throughout their march was from their airborne allies. Both Germans and their prisoners learned early to dive fast for the ditches or over walls.

It was on this march that Jack Fairweather experienced the first of many actions that would later dictate his professional career. Following one of the many strafings he dedicated himself to caring for the wounded, no matter whether prisoner or captor.

In one instance he was about to pick up a dead prisoner, to carry him to the group grave they had prepared, only to discover that the back of the man's head had be severed. When he went to lift him the brains slid out on the ground. Fairweather carefully bandaged the head with a towel, the brains restored, before taking him to burial.

"I still remember that day vividly," Veness said. "It was the first but not the last time I would see Jack drenched in the blood of others."

Once they had arrived at their first destination, a prisoner-of-war camp at Rennes, France, some of the officers were still under the impression that the Second World War was a gentleman's war. They found it difficult to adjust to the fact that after running around and shooting at the enemy they were not going back to the comfort of the Mess.

Initially the camp at Rennes was a reasonable existence, to the extent that an American Paratrooper sergeant demanded that an American Colonel insist that "the damn Krauts provide some of the luxuries to which we were accustomed."

Often the men who, like the two Jacks, had been captured on D-Day or D-Day plus One had nightmares. There would be cries in the night and some would find themselves bathed in sweat. There was fear, too, that if the SS Troops were to fall back as far as Rennes they would not hesitate to shoot every prisoner before retreating further.

The first of July they were ordered aboard box cars, almost cheek-by-jowl in a space marked "eight-horse capacity." An open bucket jammed in a corner soon permeated the air with its sickening stench.

The stench they could live with, they were not so sure that would be the case with the air attacks. Just as they had suffered from Allied air attacks during the five day march to Rennes, they now suffered constantly in fear of direct hits as bombers and fighters alike unloaded their deadly cargoes.

Macabre entertainment consisted of stories being told by pilot prisoners of the trains they had bombed and left burning before they had been shot down and captured.

The tension was terrific.

When they got to the town of Angers it was "as if a deluge of monstrous bombs had exploded in a single blast, box cars and locomotives lay about like toys thrown down by children in a temper. The loss in railway equipment was staggering, the two watchers in their car (peering through the high, narrow window slits) counted one hundred and seven wrecked engines before the vast yards had been left behind."

Veness, who had been keen on map studies, spent time studying an American flyer's silk escape map until he had memorized every detail of the surrounding countryside ... but wondered if he was too weak from lack of food to escape. The prisoners' sole fare for days had been portions of a mouldy, brick-sized loaf of black bread and brackish water.

When the train reached Tours it was caught in the middle of a major bombing raid on the railroad station: A raid that was so violent some of the prisoners were too terror-stricken to even be articulate.

They made whimpering, moaning sounds. Some tried to pray ... Fear was heavier in the car than the foul smell. There did not seem to be a chance of survival ...

The sound magnified until it seemed that the sky was filled with rushing aerial freight trains. Men squirmed against the car floor as their flesh quivered. There did not seem one chance in a million that any would survive.

Then came the dreadful 'crump, crump, crump' of bomb blasts far to the rear, and the trembling prisoners realized that the bombs released almost directly over-head had been carried far beyond the train to another target.

Jack Veness sprang to the car window and looked out. The railway yard of Tours was a hell of bursting bombs.

The two Jacks gripped hands in the darkness.

'Are you ready to jump' one of them whispered.

'After this I'll do anything,' came the answer.

Thus was the pact made.

At this time the people of Tours, led by a French Florence Nightingale came to the rescue of the starving prisoners with baskets of eggs, bread, lettuce and peas. The nurse also managed to convince the Germans to increase the meagre ration of moldy black bread with an excellent barley soup, albeit shared in twenty bowls among seven hundred prisoners – each was allowed sixty seconds in which to gobble his share.

As a result, the prisoners began to feel some strength restored. Fairweather had a little extra, he was the only one who would eat the smelly French cheese, avoiding the worms inhabiting the tunnels.

Gradually the men managed to gouge out a hole at one end of the box car, covering it with a hanging first aid kit. It went undiscovered. After the train began to move again, the terror of air raids spurred their efforts until it was large enough to crawl through onto the couplings between the cars.

The two Jacks waited until one night when the train was on a slight upgrade, then took their chances jumping. Most of the prisoners they left behind wished them luck save one voice that called out, "So long, suckers!"

Neither man suffered serious injury but Fairweather lost his glasses.

Guided by the stars, and Veness' memory of the map he had studied, they took off across the fields, coming eventually to a river he identified as the Cher.

They were a well balanced team, Veness was always in a hurry but Fairweather could not be hurried with the result that their pace was steady and their instincts sound.

After swimming the river the two men walked for two days on empty stomachs, before finally taking a chance on a farm they had observed for several hours. Here they were, if anything, overfed before being seated on the crossbars of two bicycles and driven to the headquarters of the local Maquis.

Enroute they were given shelter in the village church of St. Luzillé, where they watched from the bell tower as German troops ransacked every house in the town below.

A hidden doorway led to the tower and it was immediately apparent that people had been hidden there regularly over the centuries. One inscription carved in the wall bore the date 1778.

A few more hair-raising bicycle and car drives in the night, close calls with roaming German and Milice (French collaborator police) patrols, and Fairweather and Veness were delivered to the highly militant, fre-

Soon they were among Le Coz's favourite warriors, fighting with him side-by-side as he took out marauding German troops in the surrounding villages.

• • • • • • • • • • • • • •

quently visible and violent arm of the French Resistance.

Their arrival at the Maquis headquarters was mind-boggling.

Capitaine Georges Le Coz and his band of merry men and women had carved out an almost luxurious existence in the forest. The lavishness of the furnishings, from feather mattresses and satin sheets to vintage champagne and cognac, was so impressive that the two men began to wonder if they would wake up and find it was all a dream.

A dream it was not. A nightmare from time to time ... yes.

Here they discovered 20 men who, like them, had escaped the prison train and found their way to Le Coz.

They soon learned that under Le Coz's dictator-ship harsh and violent discipline in an atmosphere of indulgence and gluttony were the order of the day.

At the time they had no choice but to stay with the Maquis. Soon they were among Le Coz's favourite warri-ors, fighting with him side-by-side as he took out ma-rauding German troops in the surrounding villages; or running with him through the forests and back roads as the Maquis broke camp with the Germans hot on their heels.

Each new campsite, however, enjoyed the same extravagance and violence as the first.

The liberation of the walled town of *Loches* (the first church was built there in the year 405) was the most successful operation participated in by the two Jacks.

It was in *Loches* that Fairweather was fitted with new glasses (complete with green rims) by a sixteen year-old boy. On Fairweather's return home, two years later, a specialist in Saint John marvelled at the accuracy of the lenses, ruefully observing the years of study he had re-quired to produce the same result.

It was here, also, that Veness and Fairweather were to be presented, Aug. 16, 1944, with the Médaille Militaire by Le Coz, in the name of de Gaulle and the Free French.

Here, too, they were first dubbed "Les deux Jacks" by an elderly English woman who had escaped from Paris to live out the war in the village of *Loches*.

Until that day all had gone well in the town's lib-eration, even to the publication of a news sheet to com-memorate the event. But the day of celebration became a day of disaster as massed German troops charged the town and the Maquis were practically decimated.

The two Jacks were among 50, out of a band of 300, to escape.

They had heard of a hidden airfield where they might be flown to England if they could reach it and decided it was time to search it out. A reluctant Le Coz let them go, arranging for their transportation and eventual escape from occupied France.

Later, after debriefing in England, the two men found the role they had been given as instructors boring and pushed for action at the front.

As platoon commanders with their old regiment they fought in Holland to clear the path to the Rhine and battled their way into enemy positions. Veness proudly captured a German general. Their promotions were rapid and they soon reached the rank of Major, Fairweather being the youngest of such rank in the Canadian army.

Along the way they were both mentioned in despatches and evaded all attempts to send them to hospital, despite head wounds. Veness was the first Canadian fighting man to enter Germany but later received multiple shrapnel wounds, ending up in hospital for four months while Fairweather continued on with his regiment in its advance into Germany.

For all the nightmares of battle on D-Day, through the terrifying march and the later terror of the prisoner train and action in Germany, the most memorable time for the men was the months of bizarre adventure they had spent with the incredible Captain Le Coz and his band of fighting Maquis.

After the war the two Jacks went on to university, Jack Fairweather to become a doctor and Jack Veness an engineer.

At the time of this writing, June of 1997, the men were meeting again in Fredericton for the annual D-Day ceremonies on June 6.

Clergy in the battlefield ... no enemies among the dead

Clergymen in the front line in wartime?

I remember that during the Second World War we took pride in the knowledge that, when a family member was killed in action, Canadians did not get cold telegrams delivered to the door: as a general rule our clergy were alerted, it was they who bore the sad news ... and it was they who stayed to help the family through its grieving.

But at the front? Clergy marching shoulder to shoulder with fighting men?

I don't remember hearing much about them doing that but I have to admit I never gave much thought to the role of the clergy in war time. I knew there were clergy in the forces and that they were called "chaplains" but that was the extent of my knowledge. In the course of my research for this book I discovered that the role they played was quiet but vital. I learned a lot about the role of the chaplain and of one New Brunswick chaplain in particular.

In the west-side entrance of St. Michael's Church in Chatham, New Brunswick there is a stained glass window bearing the insignia of the North Shore (New Brunswick) Regiment. It was placed there in memory of "all the men" in that regiment by its chaplain, Msgr. Raymond Myles Hickey, (Major, Military Cross) who dedicated six years of his life to serving the regiment during the Second World War.

Msgr. Hickey earned his Military Cross on "D" Day when he landed with his men on the beach in Normandy, on D-Day, June 6, 1944. Throughout the bloody 10-week battle of the Failaise Gap he was at their sides, and continued beside them as they battled their way across Europe.

Hickey's description of the skies the morning of June 6, as the fire of weapons between the Germans and the Allies reddened the sky for miles around is summarized in the title of his first book *The Scarlet Dawn.*

I brought it home to read and highly recommend it, so much so that I have taken the liberty of quoting a number of passages from the initial battle and other of the Monsignor's experiences. Throughout the war he helped bury no fewer than 371 members of his regiment, as well as numerous Germans and others whose fate brought them to him.

Hickey talks of how people frequently ask whether he ever missed saying his breviary, a priestly requirement which must be met save under the most extraordinary of circumstances. For Msgr. Hickey that only happened once, the day of the battle at Carpiquet.

His description of Carpiquet paints a highly emotional picture of the invasion: *That night alone we buried 40 – Carpiquet was the graveyard of the regiment. For seven days and nights the Germans shelled us, and we lost heavily. I saw reinforcements come up to us in the evening, and I would bury them the following morning. Yes, those of us who came through it will never forget that hell called Carpiquet."*

Hickey talks of how it seemed forever that the troops had been preparing to go to war, and how the restless among them began to fear that they would go back home without having fired a shot at the enemy.

Early in March of 1944 General Keller called a meeting of all Third Division Chaplains and told them, "Gentlemen, I know when anything serious is about to happen you want time to get the men ready; all I can say is, get ready; good afternoon gentlemen."

As we drove back home through the New Forest that beautiful afternoon, though the sun was warm and the cuckoo's song was echoing in the woods, we chaplains were strangely quiet; for the first time we silently agreed that the Invasion was coming.

In action the Catholic chaplains carried the Blessed Sacrament and the Holy Oils on their persons at all times. The prayers for burial were necessarily short. Although he knew the prayers by heart, Msgr. Hickey carried a little book with him throughout the war. Its pages were torn and tattered and the words blotted with rain, mud and blood stains but later, read-ing them often brought back the days when, *ankle deep in mud, while the sky wept and wept, or at night as the flares lit up the sky with their sickening glare, or maybe in a quiet field back of the firing line, I stood by a row of rough hewn graves and read almost to myself:*

"May the angels lead thee into paradise, may the martyrs receive thee at thy coming, and lead thee into the Holy City of Jerusalem. May the choirs of angels receive thee, and mayest thou have eternal rest with Lazarus who once was poor."

This would be followed by the prayers for the dead. Hickey said that often, perhaps as he was read-ing those prayers, someone back at home was num-bering the beads for the safety of her loved one. He said that although their prayers might not be answered in the way they would have wished he, as their chaplain, knew those boys went down in their graves prepared to meet their Maker.

Preparing the troops for death was, indeed, the major role of the chaplain at war and Msgr. Hickey took that preparation seriously and worked diligently at it, to the extent that when the North Shore Regiment went into battle on D Day he knew every one of his charges was prepared both for battle and for death.

A good commander, regardless of his faith, knows the value of spiritual things when his men are preparing for battle.

Hickey's responsibilities went well beyond his own regiment. He was responsible for the Catholics in the Queens Own Rifles of Toronto, The Eighth Brigade Headquarters, a Company of the Cameron Highlanders of Ottawa, the Eighth Brigade Workshops and a Company of the Sixteenth Field Engineers ... and they were spread miles apart!

"Now Father," said Colonel Sprague of the Queen's Own Rifles, after I had finished Mass there the day before the Invasion, "have you seen all my Catholic boys?"

"Sir," I said, "there's not a sin left in your regiment, at least among the Catholics."

He laughed heartily and called the chaplain of the regiment, Capt. Clough, a good Anglican, who assured us the same could be said of the Protestants.

I wasn't surprised, because I knew the Protestant chaplains to be a fine, hard working group, and they had their men well prepared for the Invasion.

I've never felt more satisfied in my life than the night before the Invasion; for, like all the other chaplains, I had the consolation to know that every one of my men had been personally contacted and given an opportunity to receive the Sacraments. Already our hard work was reaping its reward.

I think I am expressing what most men felt the morning of the Invasion, when I saw that I wished I could always be as ready for death as I was that morning. While preparing the men, I had not forgotten my own soul; for I realized what every man who has ever gone into action realizes, that only readiness to meet death can give you courage to face it.

Msgr. Hickey was born in Jaquet River. He died June 19, 1987 in Carpiquet, France while with the men whom he had served and who loved him dearly. The veterans of the North Shore (New Brunswick) Regiment were in Carpiquet for the unveiling of a monument at the site of their major confrontation with the Germans during the battle of Falaise Gap in 1944.

Friends said that when Msgr. Hickey started out on this trip back to Carpiquet he knew it might lead to his death. He was eighty-two years old, had suffered a heart attack and was not at all well.

Ironically a monument, seven feet high and three and one-half feet across, made of Normandy granite and placed in the village square of the rebuilt village, honouring the North Shore Regiment was to be unveiled on the day he died.

Msgr. Hickey wrote a second book, *D-Day Memories*, in 1980, following the 35th anniversary of the Normandy invasion.

Distinguished Conduct Medal

*(created December 4, 1854, because of the
Crimean War and was first awarded to
a Canadian on April 19, 1901)*

Terms: The DCM was awarded to Warrant Officers, non-commissioned officers, and men, serving in any of the sovereign's military forces, for distinguished conduct in the field. It was thus the second highest award for gallantry in action (after the Victoria Cross) for all army ranks below commissioned officers and was available to navy and air force personnel also for distinguished conduct in the field.

Bars: A silver, laurelled bar was awarded for a subsequent act or acts of distinguished conduct in the field.

Description: A circular, silver medal, 1.42 inches in diameter.

Obverse: **King Edward VII**: uncrowned, in Field Marshal's uniform, facing left, with the legend EDWARDVS VII REX IMPERATOR.

King George V: uncrowned, in field Marshal's uniform facing left, with the legend GEORGEIVS V BRITT: OMN: REX ET IND: IMP.

King George VI: (a) A crowned effigy, facing left, with the legend: GEORGE IVS VI D: G: BR: OMN: REX ET INDIAE IMP: (for WWII): (b) A crowned effigy, facing left, with the legend: GEORGE1VS VI DEI GRA: BRITT: OMN: REX FID: DEF: (for Korea) BIU.

Reverse: shows FOR DISTINGUISHED/CON-DUCT/IN THE FIELD in four lines, with a horizontal line through a small oval wreath below the wording. Some Edward VII medals had the word CANADA above the inscription.

Mounting: An ornate scroll suspender is attached to the medal by a single-toe claw.

Naming: The regimental or equivalent number, rank, initials, surname and unit of the recipient are impressed in plain block capitals around the rim of the medal.

Ribbon: The crimson ribbon is 1.25 inches wide with a dark blue central stripe (0.375 inches).

Military Medal
instituted March 25, 1916

Terms: The medal is awarded to Warrant Officers, non-commissioned officers and men for individual or associated acts of bravery on the recommendation of a Commander-in-Chief in the field.

Bar: The silver, laurelled bar is awarded for a subsequent act or acts of bravery and devotion under fire.

Description: A circular, silver medal, 1.42 inches in diameter.

Obverse: **King George V**: A bareheaded effigy, in Field Marshal's uniform, facing left, and the legend: GEORGEIVS V BRITT: OMN: REX ET IND: IMP:

King George VI: A crowned effigy, facing left, and one of the legends: (a) GEORGEIVS VI D: G: BR: OMN: REX ET INDIAE IMP: (for WWI) (b) GEORGEIVS VI DEI GRA: BRITT: OMN: REX FID: DEF: (for Korea).

Queen Elizabeth II: A crowned effigy, facing right, and the legend: ELIZABETH II D: G; BR: OMN: REGINA R: D: (for Korea).

Reverse: Shows FOR/ BRAVERY/ IN THE/ FIELD in four lines encircled by a laurel wreath and surmounted by the Royal Cypher and Imperial Crown.

Mounting: An ornate scroll suspender is attached to the medal with a single-toe claw.

Ribbon: A dark blue ribbon, 1.25 inches wide, with five equal centre stripes of white, red, white, red, and white (0.125 inches each).

Naming: The regimental or equivalent number, rank, initials, surname and unit of the recipient appear in plain block capitals around the edge of the medal.

C.S.M Earl Upton, Minto

Sgt. J.C. Sansom Fredericton

Two area veterans honoured at a gala ceremony in Fredericton

Just after the Second World War, either in December of 1945 or early in 1946, the first investiture of Canadian soldiers in New Brunswick and by New Brunswick's Lieutenant-Governor, took place in Fredericton.

It was a wonderfully gala affair attended by Brigadier D.R. Agnew, Officer Commanding, New Brunswick Military Area, the Lieutenant-Governor's Aides-de-Camp, various cabinet ministers and dignitaries with their wives whose gowns of regal glory were befitting the pomp and circumstance of the occasion. The members of the armed forces, to be singled out and honoured for their wartime acts of courage, wore simple battle dress and the ribbons of battle.

Among those honoured that day were Sergeant-Major D.E. (Old Bones) Upton of Minto and Sergeant J.C. Sansom of Fredericton.

CSM Earl Upton, MM, DCM honoured for 'acts of courage' in two World Wars

Earl Upton was a Sergeant-Major with all the qualities of strictness and duty the rank of Sergeant-Major is expected to encompass. He was reputed to be a tough, but fair, taskmaster throughout his army career that spanned two world wars.

Unfortunately, despite considerable digging, records from the *First World War* reflecting the actions which led to CSM Upton receiving the Military Medal have so far eluded me.

His *Second World War* award, the Distinguished Conduct Medal, the highest honour other than a Victoria Cross that a non-commissioned officer could receive, was presented to him that day in Fredericton. The particulars of the action that precipitated the award were well documented by the late Dr. Robert Tooley in *Invicta*, the official history of the Carleton & York Regiment in the *Second World War.*

The action took place in Italy on the main road through the Liri Valley leading to Rome on what was called the Hitler Line.

The twenty-third of May dawned cloudy and the weather changed to rain in the afternoon and evening ......

...... Soon after crossing the start line A Company ran into enemy fire which fatally wounded the company

*commander, Capt. James Crook. Lieut H.J. Haining took over temporary command of the company. Despite the unremitting pounding to which it was subjected by mortars, Nebelwerfers and artillery firing from behind the Line, B Company under the cool leadership of Major Burton Kennedy was through the wire and consolidating on its objective within 75 minutes of starting ... .
in fact, Lieut Charles Kennedy's platoon, forming B Company's left flank, inadvertently advanced several hundred yards too far forward into what would be the beaten zone of the artillery concentration planned to support the WNSR in the second phase of the attack, and had to withdraw to a safer position.*

As so often happened, communications within the Battalion were hampered by the erratic performance of the portable Number 18 radio sets: B Company, whose own set had failed was able to maintain spasmodic touch with Battalion HQ through a set brought forward by Pte. Edgar Jamieson, who accompanied a group of A Company men who were making their way forward after the disorganisation of their company at the start line, until he was sent off to rejoin his own company, where he was wounded.

Meanwhile A Company had joined forces with the shrunken D Company, depleted by its casualties of the day before, and, under the command of Major Rowland Horsey, secured its objective to the right of B Company. The successful completion of A Company's consolidation on the objective, despite the disorganisation created early in the attack by enemy fire and the death of the company commander, owed much to the determined leadership of CSM Earl "Bones" Upton who was rewarded with the DCM.

When a heavy enemy counter barrage dispersed

Company HQ and separated it from the forward pla-
toons with whom contact was lost, CSM Upton reorgan-
ised company HQ, collected the reserve platoon, and,
under severe enemy artillery and mortar fire, led the
group forward to join up with the forward platoons on
the objective.

CSM Upton returned to Minto after the war but he left his heart in the Highlands of Scotland according to his niece, Kay Thurrott.

"He was Uncle Earl to everyone," she said. "Contrary to the image of the demanding Sergeant Major, Earl Upton was a very placid and quiet person at home, always there to help anyone in need."

His widowed sister was left with a young family, Mrs. Thurrott said that rather than leave her to cope all alone "Uncle Earl" remained in Canada, a bachelor until the day he died, at the age of ninety-six.

An interesting side-bar to this story is that the same sister, Marion M. Upton, that he came home to help became the Mayor of Minto, the first woman mayor in New Brunswick.

Sgt. Jim Sansom of Nashwaak Bridge cited for personal gallantry, leadership

Della Sansom dropped me a note in March of 1997 telling me that she believed her husband, Jim, was perhaps one of the stories I was looking for to include in this book. How right she was ... and how modest her husband is about his achievements.

I called him to get a few more details to add to the following citation which read:

Sgt. James Carmen Sansom,

No.7 Cdn Anti Tank Regiment, RCA

Award: The Military Medal

Citation: For personal gallantry, leadership and devotion to duty throughout the Italian & N.W. Europe Campaigns, particularly at Ravenna, Italy, 15 Sep 1944, where Sgt. Sansom personally rescued and evacuated comrades wounded when their self-propelled gun was hit, then himself took command of the gun assisted only by the driver, until the successful attack was completed. By the KING'S Order the name of

Sergeant James Carmen Sansom, Royal Canadian Artillery, was published in the London Gazette on

10 January 1946 as mentioned in a Despatch for distinguished service.

I am charged to record

His Majesty's high appreciation.

J.J. Lawson

Secretary of State for War

His reply was typical of the man:

"I will try to add a bit more to the information you already have. Please do not try to expand on the hero stuff."

The "hero stuff" does not need to be expanded on, Sgt. Sansom, it stands alone very nicely, thank you.

The following is his story:

This particular battle was one of many from Sicily to the Po River.

We were Corp troop and never knew who we would be supporting – on this occasion we were with the British Tanks and Infantry #12 Tanks and our 12 SP and Infantry. Total personnel maybe 2,000.

On our right flank and left flank maybe likewise forces.

Due to foul-ups we were caught in the open at daylight under German guns when we should have been across the valley and stream. The tanks and infantry and a few of our SP were given a mauling.

My first SP crew, Sgt. and Bombardier were wounded, the two gunners were killed.

I don't think that I did anything that any other soldier wouldn't have done under the circumstances.

How many the British crews lost, I would not know."

On Sgt. Sansom's discharge certificate the following is included in the section *Medals, Decorations, Mentions, awarded in respect of service during this war:* Military Medal; Mentioned in Despatches; 1939-45 Star; Italy Star; France and German Star; Defence Medal; Canadian Volunteer Service Medal and Clasp.

That's a fair amount of weight to carry around one's chest!

Following the war Sgt. Sansom worked for the Department of Natural Resources for ten years before going on to work for Nashwaak Pulp and Paper Company for 21 years, retiring as Assistant Manager.

On the occasion of the Diamond Jubilee of the Royal Canadian Legion Beaverbrook Branch #80 he was presented with a Life Membership with the following citation:

The Charter President of Beaverbrook Branch he has been an active member for over forty years and maintains an active interest in the branch and Legion affairs. Currently a member of the Branch Past Presidents Club. Attends all Legion functions. A well known and respected member of his community, a leader and a credit to any organization.

Our high-flying heroes
of two World Wars

The following medals were awarded to members of the Royal Canadian Air Force until 1972, at which time they were replaced by the *Cross of Valour, the Star of Courage and the Medal of Bravery* all of which are awarded to armed forces personnel and civilians alike in instances of merit.

Distinguished Flying Cross
established June 3, 1918

Terms: Awarded to Officers and Warrant Officers for an act or acts of valour, courage or devotion to duty performed while flying in active operations against the enemy.

Bars: For additional acts of bravery silver bar with an eagle in the centre is awarded.

Obverse: Cross flory terminated in the horizontal and base bars with bombs, the upper bar terminating with a rose, surmounted by another cross composed of aeroplane propellers charged in the centre with a roundel within a wreath of laurels, a rose winged ensigned by an Imperial Crown, thereon the letters RAF.

Reverse: Royal Cypher above the date 1918 in a circle: year of issue on lower arm.

Description: Cross flory, two and one-eighth inches across, silver.

Mounting: Ring at top of cross attached to the suspender by a small ring.

Ribbon: One and one-quarter inches: Violet and white alternate diagonal stripes one-eighth inch at 45 degrees left to right. The violet colour is to appear in the bottom left and upper right corners when viewed on the wearer's chest. Until 1919, the stripes were horizontal.

Air Force Cross
established June 3, 1918

Terms: Awarded to Officers and Warrant Officers for an act or acts of valour, courage or devotion to duty whilst flying but not in active operations against an enemy.

Bar: For additional acts of bravery (same bar as to DFC)

Obverse: A thunderbolt in the form of a cross, the arms conjoined by wings, the base bar terminating with a bomb surmounted by another cross composed of aeroplane propeller, the four ends enscribed with letter G (top) R (left), V (bottom), 1 (right). Current Royal Cypher has E II R with the bottom blank. In the centre is a rounded, thereon, a representative of Hermes mounted on a hawk in flight bestowing a wreath. The whole is ensigned by an Imperial Crown.

Reverse: Royal Cypher above date 1918 in a circle. Year of award appears on lower arm from 1939 on. Issued unnamed.

Description: Silver cross, one and five-eighths inches across.

Mounting: A small link at the top of the crown attaches to a slot in two sprigs of laurel. Laurel is attached to the bottom of a straight clasp.

Ribbon: One and one-quarter inches: Red and White alternate diagonal stripes one-eighth of an inch at 45 degrees left to right. The red colour is to appear in the bottom left and upper right corners when viewed on the wearer's chest. The stripes were originally horizontal but were changed in 1919.

Distinguished Flying Medal
established June 3, 1918

Terms: Awarded to non-commissioned officers and men for an act or acts of exceptional valour, courage or devotion to duty while flying in active operations against the enemy.

Bars: for additional acts of bravery, as for DFC.

Obverse: 1. George V, uncrowned coinage head, facing left. 2. George VI uncrowned coinage head facing left.

Reverse: Within a wreath of laurel, a representation of Athena Nike seated on an aeroplane, a hawk rising from her right arm above the words FOR COURAGE.

Description: Oval, one and one-eighth inches, silver.

Mounting: A bomb attached to the clasp and ribbon by two wings.

Ribbon: One and one-quarter inches. Violet and white alternate bars, one-sixteenth of an inch wide at 45 degree angle left to right. (Until July 1919 the bars were horizontal).

British Empire Medal
established August, 1917, amended 1922,
amended 1940, amended 1957.

The British Empire Medal was introduced in 1917 as part of the *Order of the British Empire* for those who have rendered important services to the Empire. In 1918 a military division was created for all commissioned, warrant and subordinate officers of the military services.

In 1922 the medal was divided into the *Medal of the Most Excellent Order of the British Empire* for Gallantry (known as the *EGM–Empire Gallantry Medal*) and the *Medal of the Most Excellent Order of the British Empire*, for Meritorious Service (BEMM). The EGM was superseded by the *George Cross* in September 1940.

The BEM continued to be awarded for meritorious service after 1940 but also for gallantry. Military and civilian divisions continued.

Bars: Awarded for additional acts of gallantry (silver laurelled bar). After 1957, a silver emblem of two oak leaves was awarded with the medal when it was awarded for gallantry. The oak leaves would also be worn on the ribbon in undress. In undress, the recipient of a bar wears a rosette. (No bars have been awarded to Canadians but the Oak Leaves have been.)

Obverse: Britannia seated with sun to her right. Legend around the edge reads FOR GOD AND THE EMPIRE and in exergue (below) is the inscription FOR MERITORIOUS SERVICE. EGM had FOR GALLANTRY in exergue.

Reverse: Royal Cypher surmounted by a crown with the words: INSTITUTED BY/ KING GEORGE V with a border of four heraldic lions.

Description: Circular, 1.42 inches, silver. A thin medal.

Mounting: A straight clasp attached to the medal by laurel leaves.

Ribbon: 1917-37; one and one-sixteenth inches. Purple (military had a central thin red stripe). From 1937 on one and one-quarter inches. Rose pink ribbon edged with thin pearl grey stripes. Military has central thin grey stripe added.

Canada's super fighting pilots of the First World War were famous

One of Canada's most highly decorated airmen during the First World War was Major Albert DesBrisay Carter from Pointe de Bute. What he may have achieved with an earlier start on active duty can only be imagined. What he did achieve, in the four and one-half months after he arrived in France at the end of 1917, is nothing short of amazing.

Carter was yet another Canadian super fighting pilot. He gunned down no fewer than 32 German aircraft in those few short months before being downed himself and ending up a prisoner of war.

Just for comparison's sake it's interesting to note that Eddie Rickenbacker, of U.S. fame in the same war, only chalked up 25 "kills."

Carter, on the other hand, was a straggler by Canadian standards, when compared to Billy Bishop's 72 planes and Collishaw's 60.

Carter was awarded the Distinguished Service Order medal, with Bar, and the government of France awarded him a Croix de Guerre. One medal citation noted that he distinguished himself with "great keenness and dash, ranging far behind the German lines in his versatile Sopwith Dolphin, and strafing ground troops at such low levels that they ducked in panic."

Ironically, after surviving so many close brushes with death, it was a German plane that ultimately killed him ... After the war!

When the Germans turned over their remaining aircraft to the Allies in 1918 Major Carter, as did other pilots, had the opportunity to own one of the planes for his personal use. Carter chose a Fokker Flying Scout, telling everyone he preferred it to the British and French war planes.

One day in 1919 he took the Fokker up for the entertainment of friends, who watched from the ground as he displayed his flying skills. All went well for a time until he tried to put the German aircraft through a sudden twist. The twist was too much for the Fokker's otherwise strong structure and, as the horror-stricken spectators watched, the plane suddenly disintegrated sending the great war flier to his death.

'Sometimes I find myself waiting for Donnie to buzz us'
Don Dickson, DFC, AFC, DFM, BEM

Someone must have noticed that young Don Dickson was no ordinary individual, long before he began buzzing the family farmhouse at Hammond River.

His brother Lawrence, who still lives in the 140 year old family home, was already suspicious and school chums found him a bit of a daredevil. They still chuckle about the day, back in the late 1930s, when Don was expelled from high school.

"Once we passed out of the local one-room school we had to go down to Rothesay, a village about 10 miles away, if we wanted to go on to high school. Back in those days families didn't have cars, precious few farmers even had trucks so we travelled by milk train (it stopped to pick up milk from the farmers along the way). In the afternoon we waited around in the school until five o'clock to ride the same train back home at night.

"Waiting around made it easy to get up to mischief. Like the day a bunch of us were looking out our classroom window at the Girl Guides lining up for a parade down below. One of the girls suddenly ran up behind Don and jumped on his back. He turned around quick and grabbed for her but all he caught was her skirt, pulling open the zipper that was holding it up. She spun around, the skirt dropped to the floor, Don grabbed it and, like a flash, tossed it out the window on top of one of the Girl Guides.

"The family sent him to a private school but he never did get to graduate, life held too many other interesting things to do. He was always in a hurry, no car ever went fast enough to suit him so it was no surprise to anyone when he enlisted in the RCAF in October of 1940. He was 20 years old."

The RCAF discovered Donald's talent as a pilot very early.

"He could do just about anything with an aeroplane. He almost got court marshalled once for flying the Saskatchewan River at water level and jumping the bridges."

But instead of getting court-marshalled the high spirited Donald, by now better known as "Dickie" to his Air Force friends, kept picking up medals along the way.

On Sept. 1, 1942 he was promoted to Pilot Officer and the *Telegraph Journal* reported the following:

"Flight Sergeant John (sic) (*James is correct, dd*) Donald Dickson, who acted as captain of the aircraft 26 times was awarded the Distinguished Flying Medal for great gallantry in the performance of his duty while serving with No. 57 Squadron of the RAF and promoted to the rank of Pilot Officer.

The Citation reads: *He executed his tasks with the utmost vigour and determination. Undeterred by bad weather, he makes every effort to locate the target and bomb it accurately. On one occasion over Stuttgart he descended to 3,000 feet to ensure success. He partici-*

pated in attacks on Brest, Hamburg, Rostock, Essen, Emden and many equally important targets.

Throughout those 26 missions his lucky talisman was a Victory Loan Pennant from a Kings County Victory Bond Campaign which had exceeded its quota with "flying colours." It was presented to him by George Hamm, a member of the campaign who was staying the summer at a farm next door to the Dickson's.

On Oct. 14, that same year he was listed as "dangerously injured on active service overseas, suffering from lacerations of the scalp and concussion."

Following this injury Dickson proceeded to wear his cap at a jaunty, non regulation, angle to cover the scar over his left eye, the only visible reminder of what his mother referred to as "the bad time" he and the pennant had in the waters of the English Channel.

An artist's concept in the *Telegraph Journal* on Oct. 23, 1942, shows the Victory Torch pennant emblazoned on the side of a Canadian bomber, flaunting its challenge over Nazi Germany during an air attack on industrial Essen.

It was on Dickson's second tour of duty in 1943 that his talents as a pilot hit the headlines across the country. Rudy Wagner of Edmonton, Alta. was gunnery leader of the squadron at the time and, in a letter to Lou Duffley, historian and boyhood friend of Dickson's, Wagner called him "one of the finest pilots, the most courageous and completely competent airman I have ever known."

Reports of the following dog-fight ... that should have been a disastrous (for the bomber) battle between a cumbersome Halifax Bomber and two enemy fighter aircraft ... were carried in newspapers across Canada.

Dickson's Moose Squadron Halifax had dumped

Artist's rendering of the Victory Loan pennant replicated on Dickson's fuselage through 26 missions.
● ● ● ● ● ● ● ● ● ● ● ● ● ● ●

death by the ton on Hamburg and was flying out of the target area when the night fighter emerged out of the darkness in front of the bomber.

Wagner, who was manning the two machine guns in the front turret spotted the attacker first and shouted "Night-fighter ahead! Dive to port" over the intercom.

"I heard his gun rattle twice," said Flt. Sgt. Jimmy Allan, "and then the RAF bomb aimer shouted 'You've got him'. The skipper was banking our Halifax to port in the meantime and we could see the Messerschmitt falling. It blew three times on the way down. When it hit the deck its flares started shooting out."

Then, as they were flying over the Nazi island stronghold of Heligoland, an even more exciting combat occurred.

Once more Wagner was the first to spot the attacker, an unidentified night-fighter carrying a search-light in the nose. It twisted ahead of the bomber, apparently playing decoy.

Wagner fired steadily at it, while the skipper tried to manoeuvre the Halifax so that the rear gunner could get in some bursts. Something must have gone wrong with the decoy business, because the night fighter finally attacked alone, diving down head-on at the four engine bomber.

"Jerry was coming at high speed and dead for us from about 1,000 feet above. I had his nose dead in my sights and he flew straight down the path of my bullets. I think I killed the pilot, for the fighter came straight at us and made no effort to pull out. He didn't fire a shot," Wagner said.

Dickson said he had to yank the control column back all the way to avoid it and the Halifax literally "stood on its tail," wavered and fell over on its back.

Inside the bomber Dickson found himself sitting on the bomb aimer. The Scot navigator was rolling around the ceiling and Allan dropped headfirst into the astro-dome. Luckily he didn't go through the perspex. As the Halifax lurched into a spin he found himself thrown back on the floor, then up to the ceiling again.

Dickson nursed the huge aircraft back into level flight after it had fallen only 4,000 feet. The rear gunner reported later that the port engine of the night fighter was in flames as the Nazi dived out of sight.

"A motor conked out as we came out of the spin and we flew home on three," Dickson said later.

The only injury to the Canadian crew was to the rear gunner who was knocked out during the fall. His turret was spinning and he was spinning inside it.

A Distinguished Flying Cross
from the King's Hands at Buckingham Palace

According to a Canadian Press Cable News story datelined London, March 31, the investiture of eight members of the RCAF took place at Buckingham Palace and Dickson was one of two to receive the Distinguished Flying Cross "from the King's Hands."

His citation reads: "This officer has taken part in a large number of flying operations. He has penetrated the defences of the Ruhr on 18 occasions in addition to participating in attacks on Berlin, Hamburg and Rostock.

"In March, 1943, in the Bremen area his aircraft was attacked by a Messerschmidt 110. The enemy fighter was destroyed by the front gunner. Shortly after another attack was made by a Junkers 88. During the combat which ensued P.O. Dickson again displayed outstanding airmanship and again furnished his gunners with opportunities for retaliation.

"His skill undoubtedly made a safe return possible. P.O. Dickson's sustained gallantry over a very long period has been most meritorious."

Most men would be content with seeing such action but Don Dickson was made of different stuff than most men. He continued serving his second tour of action then proceeded to instruct other pilots, teaching them the skills that constantly brought his crews home safely.

To the top of the world!

By 1945, however, Squadron Leader Dickson was off on yet another adventure, called Operation Musk-Ox.

Three New Brunswickers, Dickie Dickson along with Flying Officer W. M. Allwood, from Saint John, and Chief Navigation Officer Jim Roper of Moncton were called on to become part of Canada's famous Musk-Ox Expedition. They were scheduled to spend five months in the Arctic northland in combined operations manoeuvres, testing new equipment and military conditions under the severest winter weather.

Jim Roper later noted that he knew of Dickson at the time as being considered "very serious and professional as a pilot.

"He was gifted with much good humour and extremely well liked by all who knew him."

Lawrence Dickson says his brother must have been miserable at the prospect of going to the Arctic because there was nothing in the world he hated more than cold weather.

There were twelve Vampire jets and an undisclosed number of North Stars ... each carrying 50 ground crew personnel and 10,000 pounds of servicing equipment ... involved in the project.

Col. (Ret.) R.C. Bayliss wrote to Dickson's boyhood friend Lou Duffley giving a brief insight into his involvement with Dickson in the project and, later in England.

"The story starts in Churchill on Jan. 8, '46,"

Bayliss said. "The army had developed snowmobiles that could carry half a dozen troops and tow a sled full of supplies. The air force would keep them supplied, either by air drop or caches, as they travelled north to Cambridge Bay, west to Aklavik, and south to Dawson City.

"Don was one of the eight Dakota captains and a fine one at that. It didn't matter if the landing strip was gravel or just a cleared strip on a lake, frozen of course, Don would grease the plane down with the greatest of ease. One time at Fort Simpson the snow was pretty deep, landing was no problem but we wondered about the take-off. No problem either, half flap and full power and we soared into the air."

The expedition was plagued with difficulties, primarily with snowmobile breakdowns. The RCAF were kept busy supplying them with new motors, entailing many a hairy landing in the snow-covered wilderness.

Lawrence tells the story of how during one of these expeditions his brother's plane ran into a severe snow storm and he was flying more than just blind. One of the crew had dropped the gyro compass, in itself bad enough in the circumstances, but it was compounded by the fact that they couldn't raise anyone at the airport radio control tower to get guidance that way. The crew was ready to abandon the plane to the unknown tundra below but the pilot would have none of it.

"He said there was no way he was going to bale out of a warm plane into a snow bank unless there was no other alternative."

The only alternative was, of course, to rely on Dickie Dickson's flying skills and pilot's instincts.

He dropped the aircraft down low, under the weather, and nursed it along until he saw what he believed to be a familiar coastline and followed it, landing safely a short time later in a small northern airport. There he discovered that the reason the crew's calls hadn't been answered had nothing to do with the storm or a communications breakdown ... but everything to do with the fact that the control tower crew were all watching a movie.

Following the Operation Musk-Ox adventure Dickson participated in a joint Canada United States pioneer project, a military exercise called "Sweetbrier" before joining the United Nations airlift in aid of South Korea and, once more, to be honoured by Royalty. This time by Queen Elizabeth II.

KOREA Citation 19812
Squadron Leader Donald Dickson DFC DFM

Squadron Leader Dickson has served on the Korean Airlift as captain of a North Star aircraft since its inception, being a member of 426 Transport Squadron which was attached to the Military Air-Transport Service, USAF, on July 26, 1950. He has flown a total of 600 hours over the 11,000 nautical mile route, often through hazardous icing and fog conditions, without mishap. This is a direct reflection of his exceptional ability, resourcefulness and leadership.

This officer was recently appointed second in command of the squadron and is now directly responsible for all RCAF operations over the Pacific. His sterling qualities and ability as a pilot were demonstrated forcibly on a flight from McChord Air Force Base, Washington, to Elmendorf Air Force Base, Alaska on the 23rd November.

As on all trips, the aircraft was loaded with troops

and vital supplies for the United Nations effort in Korea. After completing two hours of the eight hour flight the aircraft encountered most severe icing conditions and head winds. In spite of the weather Squadron Leader Dickson completed his flight, landing at his destination in a 74 knot gale.

All other aircraft flying the route that encountered the same conditions, with the exception of another RCAF aircraft, aborted and returned to their points of departure. Had it not been for the superior skill and determination shown by this officer a vital load would have been delayed.

Squadron Leader Dickson's qualities of leadership are an inspiring example to the officers and airmen under his command and his untiring efforts have been an outstanding contribution to the success of the Royal Canadian Air Force's participation in this operation.

The Queen's Birthday Honours list special Korean section awarded the Air Force Cross to Squadron Leader James D. Dickson, DFC, DFM. After service on the airlift he became second in command of 412 Transport Squadron at Ottawa's Rockliffe Airport.

There were some perks in the airlift job, however, he confided to Lawrence. Among them was the opportunity to stop over in Honolulu (at the slightest excuse) on regular flights to Japan.

One stopover seemed justified, initially. He told Lawrence that as he was approaching the Hawaiian Islands the aircraft began to give him trouble, he couldn't seem to keep it in trim. He advised the airport that he would be landing there then went to the back of the aircraft to see if he could determine what was causing the problem.

The solution was right in front of him: One of the crew had bought his son a bicycle when he was in Japan and was riding it around the empty cargo space. Dickson dropped in at Honolulu anyway.

Peacetime continued to offer
challenge and excitement

Dickson's newest challenge was to be the designated captain of the first British Comet jet airliner to be delivered to a commonwealth air force, the RCAF. After training in England and expeditions such as flying the Comet from London to Johannesburg, a distance of 6,270 miles, he was considered properly prepared for the flight across the Atlantic.

The trip marked the first time a commercial jet flew across the Atlantic, arriving in Iceland four hours and 22 minutes after leaving London, despite strong headwinds.

The Comet's debut in Canada, carrying a contingent of press and radio reporters, took place in June of 1953 in what was then considered a phenomenal, 57 minute, flight from Ottawa to New York.

The last time Lawrence saw his brother was the day Ed. Titus from Saint John ("He was as much of a daredevil as Don,") landed a Liscomb Aircraft in the field in front of the Dickson farm. Don had flown the Comet to Moncton and was ferried to Hammond River by Titus, in time to be Lawrence's best man at his wedding.

It was not long after that, while continuing to fly the Comet around the world, that he was taken ill in Newfoundland, enroute to England. At the time it was thought that he was suffering from a cold and he was allowed to continue to England. He was described as being "deathly ill" by the time he arrived. On July 25,

1953 he died from poliomyelitis. He was 32 years old.

Donald Dickson was a natural hero. He took great pleasure in life and lived it well.

One of the saddest notes in his story is the fact that, despite his wishes, his remains could not be brought home to the family burial plot in Hammond River, New Brunswick.

It was, and still is, against Canadian military regulations.

Donald Dickson, DFC, AFC, DFM and British Empire Medallist, was buried in the cemetery at the fighter base in North Luffenham, England.

Nearly 20 years later, when the Rothesay Branch of the Royal Canadian Legion was rebuilt in Rothesay, New Brunswick, its new hall was dedicated in 1972 to Donald Dickson. A charcoal portrait of this outstanding RCAF pilot remains today as a memorial.

But perhaps the most aesthetic memorial for his only living brother is remembering when, during the Korean War, Don Dickson was instructing RCAF pilots at nearby Pennfield Air Base in Charlotte County (by then just a short skip and a jump over the lush valleys of the St. John and Kennebecasis rivers to where the salmon still spawn in the Hammond River).

"He would buzz the farmhouse on a regular basis and every time he did it Mother maintained she wasn't going to run out 'this time' and wave her tea towel ... but she always did!

"Many a time we'd be just sitting down to Sunday dinner when we'd hear him and she'd jump up and away she'd go, laughing. Sometimes today, when we sit down to Sunday dinner, I find myself listening. Waiting for Donnie to buzz us."

Fredericton Wing Commander takes squadron on North Sea sub chase

The Royal Canadian Air Force Coastal Command's close association with Royal Navy operations during the Second World War is noted in the introduction to section one of *The RCAF Overseas – the Fifth Year* (September 1943 to August 1944 segment of the official history of the RCAF, published in 1945 by Oxford Press).

"Because of the secrecy which necessarily enshrouds naval dispositions and merchant shipping movements, the work of this branch of the air force receives much less publicity than that of the other Commands.

"A smashing attack on Berlin by our bombers, or the rout of a Luftwaffe formation by the fighting boys is immediately front page news; but the shepherding safely to port, through sub-infested waters, of a convoy of 50 or more ships laden with the very lifeblood of Allied existence is all in the day's work for coastal crews."

The history goes on to note that had the U-boat threat in the Atlantic succeeded, the Allies would not have been hammering at the gates of Germany by 1945.

"At best we should have been forced to accept a stalemate and a negotiated peace, leaving the Nazis in control of conquered Europe."

Among the men recognized during the fight to

keep the sea-lanes to Britain open were the names of two young New Brunswick men, Wing Commander C.G.W. Chapman, D.S.O. of Fredericton and Sgt. R. Cromarty of Blissville, a member of his crew.

By September, 1943, the RCAF Eastern Air Command had managed to severely reduce U-boat activities in Canadian operations waters. As a result, United Kingdom authorities asked if one of Canada's long-range bomber reconnaissance squadrons could be despatched to Iceland, to work in submarine operations over the northern shipping routes. The squadron was to remain under the administrative control of Eastern Air Command.

The unit selected had been formed in May of 1942 and was equipped with Canso amphibians. Wing Commander Chapman, a permanent RCAF officer, was in command.

They arrived in Greenland in January of 1944. It wasn't long before the squadron began making its mark. By June, the Allies were ready for D-Day and the invasion of France and at this time W/C Chapman and his crews are reported to have chalked up "an amazing record of successes, winning among them one Victoria Cross, (the first ever awarded to the RCAF) two DSOs, seven DFCs and three DFMs in a single month.

The book outlines two particular attacks then goes on to say:

"Not to be outdone by the rest of the squadron, the C.O. accounted for the next victim, two days later. T-Tommy, his aircraft, was on a routine patrol when a U-boat was sighted just as its conning tower came to the surface.

"A low-level attack with depth charges was made

and then Chapman circled as the U-boat, with decks awash, turned slowly to starboard. After travelling for about 400 yards the sub stopped and began to settle by the bow, with her stern in the air, the rudder and motionless propellers plainly visible and many of the crew in the water. At that point, it looked like a clear-cut victory for the Canso, which made several runs to obtain photographic evidence of the kill. However, the conning tower reappeared and, as the aircraft was making another run, an enemy gunner managed to open fire to such effect that T-Tommy's hull was badly holed and the port engine hit so that it leaked oil and belched black smoke.

"The damaged engine was switched off, but the propeller could not be feathered nor the fuel jettisoned. Finally, after being forced down from 1,000 ft. to wave-top height, Chapman cut his starboard engine and ditched safely. During the 15 to 20 minutes that the flooding hull remained afloat the crew abandoned the aircraft smoothly, launched their two dinghies and even salvaged cameras, documents and maps. But luck was against them, as one of the dinghies burst on inflation and the whole crew was forced to take to the other dinghy and let the equipment go. Two crew members got into the dinghy while others held onto the sides, with the idea of taking turns. After changing places a few times the men were unable to climb into the dinghy, owing to their weakness and waterlogged clothing. All were suffering from cold.

"While ditching, the Canso had sent out an S.O.S. and a little more than an hour later a Coastal Command Liberator sighted the crew and directed A/S R Warwick to the scene."

Eventually another lifeboat was dropped and, with superhuman effort the Flight Officer, D.J.C. Waterbury swam out and succeeded in bringing the lifeboat back to his comrades. Unfortunately, one weakened member who had been held up by his companions for some time, was too weak to hold on any longer and was lost. It was nine hours before rescue arrived. By then two more members of the crew were suffering from exposure and immersion to such an extent that they could not be revived, despite persistent efforts at artificial respiration.

All the surviving members of the crew were decorated, Chapman received the DSO and Sgt. R.F. Cromarty the Distinguished Flying Medal.

Zest for life ... a common trait among New Brunswick heroes

In April of 1985, *Telegraph-Journal* columnist Don Hoyt wrote, "A producer seeking talent for a Second World War movie would have no trouble typecasting Paul Burden.

"Never mind the grey his hair and moustache have turned; Burden, at 64, looks like a dashing devil-may-care pilot who should be standing in leather jacket and silken scarf at a bar, waiting for the order to scramble for a bombing run."

Little about Paul Burden has changed in the last 12 years. Granted, a little more water has flowed under the old Fredericton highway bridge he's said to have flown his Lancaster Bomber under and there's more grey in the hair, but that effervescent, confident personality still shines through.

Burden survived 41 bombing missions in all, 20 of them with Canada's only Pathfinder Squadron, whose coveted Pathfinder "Shite Hawk" emblem he cherishes... it's been said that only one crew among 11 Pathfinders would survive 30 missions.

He doesn't remember what his citation said when he was awarded the Distinguished Flying Cross ("...it means lots and lots of aggressive war-making"). What he does remember is his last bombing mission in a

Halifax bomber, which had been converted to the lumbering four-engine Lancaster.

"Our target was Merseburg, although oddly enough history calls it a raid on Leuna. I remember it vividly for a number of reasons, one of them being that the flight was eight hours and 35 minutes long and I did the time without a pee. If that sounds strange, let me explain. It was tradition (or call it superstition?) that the last thing I did before getting into the plane for takeoff was pee on the tail wheel. I would not pee again until I could repeat the performance on a safe landing.

"My crew were a bunch of happy-go-lucky guys and on this particular briefing we had a Royal Artillery Major present, an anti-aircraft specialist. That night we were designated as supporters for the Pathfinders, whose job it was to mark out our targets and to act as targets as well. Blackburn, our Squadron Leader, had the artillery anti-aircraft major with him.

"When we got there you could have read the *Telegraph-Journal* the sky was so bright with flak. Of course the guys were throwing out tinsel which confused the anti-aircraft readings and added to the brightness. Blackburn was within sight of our plane and he and the visiting artillery major could see the barrage ... -2-3-4 ... about two city blocks from us.

"The major said, 'they're not bad, you know?' meaning the German gunners.

"We were getting ready to do our job and by then the flak was about one city block away from us, 'Jolly good shooting!' said the major of the Germans.

"By then the flak was causing ripples but we had our bomb doors open and we were committed. Up came the ... 1,2,3,4, ... again and it rocked the hell out of us. The major, watching from Blackburn's aircraft, said,

'Too bad. They missed them.' meaning too bad the Germans missed us!"

It was following this run that Burden decided to go with the Pathfinders.

"They constantly had to seek recruits," he said. "They would go around prowling for pilots, looking for the 'press-on' types. They needed gung-ho skippers and above-average navigational teams. The success or failure of the main force rested squarely on the Pathfinders."

He's proud of the fact that he never lost any of his Pathfinder crew. "Every crew that started with me survived."

Although his education and background was in agriculture Burden wanted desperately to be a pilot when he enlisted in 1940. He thinks the fact he had owned a motorcycle helped put him in the pilot's seat. For three years he ferried planes across Canada before being shipped overseas to fly the Halifax, and later, the awesome four-engine Lancaster bombers.

It was on July 30, 1945 that he decided to take a Lancaster bomber home, just to show his mother what he did during the war. Frederictonians around at that time have not forgotten the event.

The *Daily Gleaner* ran a story with the headlines:

"RCMP Carrying On Investigation Into Identity Of Pilot."

"Played Hide And Seek With Rooftops Of City on Monday."

"Mayor R.T. Forbes Says Stunting In Air Over City Must Cease."

Here is the story as recounted by Don Hoyt:

"Reaching the city shortly before one o'clock Monday afternoon, the four-motor bomber with a twin tail and topside turret swooped down over the dome of the post office and skirted the rooftops of the buildings in the centre of the business district.

"It banked deeply around two of the taller church steeples and frightened a man standing on a house roof on Argyle Street into falling off.

"During one of the plane's repeated nose dives at the city, one citizen nearly passed out."

Burden said he was being sent with a Lancaster from Scoudouc to Wright Field in Dayton, Ohio, to represent the RCAF at an American Air Force birthday celebration. He had seven air crew and three ground crew on the flight with him.

"My parents lived on Charlotte Street and I telephoned my mother from Scoudouc and told her to come out in a half-hour to see a Lancaster.

"I appeared over Fredericton with 2,000 gallons of fuel and all kinds of time so I showed all the local folks what a Lancaster looked like.

"I went over Marysville first. Some of the local citizenry got quite excited."

But Burden emphatically denies knocking any bricks off the top of the Marysville cotton mill as one journalist claimed. He does, however, admit that there was a point when he looked up at the finger pointing heavenward atop the Wilmot United Church.

Did he really fly under the Fredericton highway bridge?

"There is a difference," he told Hoyt, "between flying under the bridge and below the bridge." On that thought he added the information that on one of the two sweeps he made across the city his Lancaster went down the riverbank a foot above the St. John River.

The late Ralph Limerick has been quoted as saying that an RCMP officer claimed he had to stop his car at the corner of York and Queen streets, "to let an aircraft cross."

There were those who muttered about a court-martial for Flight Lieutenant Burden the logical culprit since his Lancaster was the only four engine RCAF aircraft in the air over Canada that day.

"It was pretty strong circumstantial evidence," he confessed. Not too many planes could be mistaken for the Lancaster with its twin tails and gun turrets sticking out everywhere and tall identification letters on its sides.

"When people found out it was a hometown boy they were a little reticent to tell all. As a matter of fact there were 34 four-engined aircraft over New Brunswick that day. Most of them were Americans coming home from Europe."

Burden went on to say that the aircraft that visited Fredericton was never identified. Then mused, nostalgically, "I could see my mother there on Charlotte Street, waving her apron."

As many New Brunswickers will remember Paul Burden returned to Fredericton and settled down ... somewhat. He, with his wife Iris, raised no fewer than eight children, five of them adopted. When I talked to him just after Easter in 1997, he was proud of the fact that seven of the children and numerous grandchildren had been either with them or in touch over the Easter weekend.

Lest visions of that devil-may-care pilot be lost in the image of a man who: founded a successful office supply business, ran twice (unsuccessfully) for Member of Parliament on the Liberal Party ticket and continues to go to work every day at Burden Auctioneers and Liquidators (son Christopher's business).

A sidebar story of note: he started in business operating a kennel where he bred and raised Bull Mastiffs from a dog he smuggled from England. He later bred and raised Peruvian Horses, as a hobby, from the parade stallion he rode daily, most notably in parades until two years ago.

Burden remains active in the Royal Canadian Legion and in the community, giving a helping hand wherever he sees a need.

A man with a zest for life.

'As a bomber pilot you had to be lucky and have a very good crew'

Flight Lieutenant Randolf Shedd, DFC, says that while he may have received a Distinguished Flying Cross for *great gallantry in performance of his duty while serving with the 426 Squadron, RCAF...*

"... the truth was that I was very lucky and had a very good crew.

"For example, I had a rear gunner with great night vision. He could see things none of the rest of us could see, most notably enemy aircraft hovering above us preparing to attack."

A lively 87 year-old, Shedd was known as "Pappy" by his younger crew members. He was 29 years-old compared to their more tender early twenties but he still vividly remembers the 37 missions of their tour of operations.

"We had some funny ones. We were carrying all high explosives, 1,000 and 2,000 pounders, and one time an anti-aircraft shell landed almost on them. It blew my bomb bay door right off, blew holes in one aileron and the right wing ... but we got home all right.

"Then there was another time when we were flying a new Halifax bomber, with those we carried bombs on the wings as well as in the body. The only problem was that the ones on the wings wouldn't release and that night we had no choice but to head back to base carrying loaded bombs with us.

"I remember it was raining and one of the returning aircraft had pranged on the runway, which meant we would have to land in a crosswind. Pretty nerve-wracking! I had the guys suit up ready to jump but they all stuck with me and, as luck would have it, I came down as smooth as silk with the bombs still intact! Needless to say we still left the plane in a hurry!"

Shedd and his crew were on all of the three biggest missions, to Berlin, Leipzig and Nuremberg. Flying the bombing runs was a death-defying mission bar none, the bomber command had the biggest casualties of the war, he said. During the Berlin run more than 55 aircraft were lost, Leipzig accounted for 57 and Nuremberg, 100.

One thousand bombers would take off from England in waves, sometimes as many as five waves. They flew in the wake of the small Pathfinder aircraft that went ahead to put down flares on the targets, distract enemy aircraft and to generally smooth the way as much as possible for the slower and more cumbersome bombers which often weighed as much as 65,000 pounds at takeoff carrying their payload of bombs.

"We'd try to get them as high as we could, so we'd be above the anti-aircraft flak," Shedd said.

"One time, after D-Day, we were lead bomber on a run to knock out the steelworks at Cannes. We just didn't know what to expect and we were ready for any-

thing. The bombers
would lay down strips of
tinsel (fine tinfoil) from
the aircraft windows from
the minute they reached
Europe. The tinsel would
cross up the enemy air-
craft and make it difficult
for them to spot us. The
only trouble was that the
lead bombers didn't have
anyone in front of them
laying down tinsel and we
didn't know what kind of
trouble we would run
into.

Dropping the payload

"Well, we needn't
have worried. The Path-
finders ahead of us had done their job well, we dropped
our payload and headed for home with no more trouble than you would have flying over the City of Saint
John."

On that particular run Shedd's aircraft was carrying one of the newest pieces of wartime technology.
It was one of the first infra-red cameras and it was
photographing their target to check where the bombs
had hit.

"We didn't have a clue what it was, we just did
what we had to do."

The philosophy among any of the air crew was
that what they were doing was a job. Nothing more
and nothing less.

"We didn't feel heroic or anything but you got

yourself up to do what you knew you had to do. If you got uptight about it you were in trouble."

Shedd flew the Lancaster bombers first and they remained his favourite aircraft.

"The pilot was out in the nose more and could see around him, the Lancaster could take a lot of punishment too and still bring you home safely."

Shedd joined the Royal Canadian Air Force in June of 1940, he received the Distinguished Flying Cross on Oct. 21, 1944, during what he claims was the worst year of the war for the RCAF.

He was slated to go East to Burma but learned he wasn't needed and returned to Canada in April of 1945.

"I was from Toronto but I liked it in the East and I had the opportunity to open the first Canadian Tire Store here, so I decided to take it."

More than 50 years later he continues to live in the suburbs of Saint John, playing golf, boating, gardening and enjoying his grandchildren.

About the Author

Dorothy Dearborn began writing as a child and published her first poetry and short stories in the 1950s. A television career in the 1960s was interrupted by six years of front-line political involvement.

She worked as a reporter and served in various editorial positions, including that of city editor, at the *Evening Times Globe* and was editor of the weekly newspapers *The Kings County Record* and the *Saint John Citizen*.

Among her many interests are the promotion of adult literacy in New Brunswick and an often frustrating romance with Duplicate Bridge.

Mrs. Dearborn continues to work as a journalist. Her work may be found in numerous regional, national and international newspapers and magazines.

When not travelling the province researching and collecting stories and information for her work she can be found in front of her Macintosh computer at the family's 19th century farmhouse in Hampton in the company of an ancient pony named Soupy and surrounded by a motley assortment of other critters including a ferocious guard rooster named Rocky.

She is married to Fred Dearborn, they have four grown children and increasing numbers of grandchildren.

About the Illustrator

Carol Taylor of Rothesay is a new Brunswick figurative artist who works primarily in clay and oil. Her most recent work, one of a triumvirate of artists' interpretations of Delta, was exhibited at the New Brunswick Museum. Carol's figurehead clock design is permanently displayed above the Germain Street entrance of the Saint John City Market.